Easy Lotus® Notes
for Windows™

Andrew Bryce Shafran

Easy Lotus Notes for Windows

Copyright © 1994 by Que® Corporation.

Library of Congress Catalog No.: 94-65891

ISBN: 1-56529-769-5

97 96 95 94   4 3 2 1

Interpretation of the printing code: the rightmost double-digit number is the year of the book's printing; the rightmost single-digit number, the number of the book's printing. For example, a printing code of 94-1 shows that the first printing of the book occurred in 1994.

Screen reproductions in this book were created with Collage Complete from Inner Media, Inc., Hollis, NH.

Publisher: David P. Ewing

Associate Publisher: Corinne Walls

Publishing Director: Lisa A. Bucki

Managing Editor: Anne Owen

Product Marketing Manager: Greg Wiegand

Credits

Publishing Manager
Lisa A. Bucki

Acquisitions Editor
Nancy Stevenson

Product Director
Steven M. Schafer

Technical Editor
Raphael Savir

Production Editor
Heather Northrup

Copy Editor
Pamela Wampler

Book Designer
Amy Peppler-Adams

Cover Designer
Jay Corpus

Production Team
Stephen Adams
Angela Bannan
Anne Dickerson
Karen Dodson
Teresa Forrester
Joelynn Gifford
Jay Lesandrini
Elizabeth Lewis
Andrea Marcum
Tim Montgomery
Nanci Sears Perry
Dennis Sheehan
Sue VandeWalle
Johnna VanHoose
Mary Beth Wakefield

Indexer
Michael Hughes

Composed in *Stone* and *MCPdigital* by Que Corporation

About the Author

Andrew Bryce Shafran is a student at Ohio State University in Columbus. He is a junior studying Computer Science Engineering. Born in Columbus, Andy has worked with Lotus Notes for approximately two years and has developed a Lotus Notes training course. His interests include computer networking, desktop publishing, software training, and Broadway musicals.

This is his first book for Que Corporation.

Acknowledgments

I owe thanks to many people who have helped me learn how to use Lotus Notes and have given me the opportunity and time to work with them. Foremost is Debbie Geldis, who gave me my original opportunity to take a peek on Notes even when I had so many other tasks to take care of; I also thank Ray Boyles for being a supportive friend who was always there to answer questions and help me out.

Special thanks go to Scott Morgan, who really opened my eyes to Notes and project management, and Gary Burnette, who gave me my first Notes-exclusive opportunity in sunny North Carolina. In addition, I thank the following Que employees: Tom Godfrey, for giving me the opportunity to write this book; Steve Schafer, for patiently answering my questions and working with me; and Heather Northrup for keeping me focused while rewriting the book. I also thank Raphael Savir for catching all my technical bugs about Note's functionality.

Finally, I would like to thank my parents for being supportive and enthusiastic about this project and my college career.

Trademark Acknowledgments

All terms mentioned in this book that are known to be trademarks or service marks have been appropriately capitalized. Que cannot attest to the accuracy of this information. Use of a term in this book should not be regarded as affecting the validity of any trademark or service mark.

Lotus Notes is a registered trademark of Lotus Development Corporation.

Microsoft Windows is a registered trademark of Microsoft Corporation.

Contents at a Glance

Contents

Part IV: Using the Full Text Search Commands 68

Part V: Using and Printing Documents 88

Part VI: Securing and Customizing the Notes Workspace 106

Part VII: Developing Notes Databases   132

Part VIII: Advanced Notes Features   160

Part IX: Glossary   184

Index   190

Action Index   198

Introduction

Notes falls under a category of software entitled *groupware*. This means that Notes' strengths make it easy to tie together various groups of people using one software package. Because it's easy to share information across the entire Notes network, Lotus Notes is a popular vehicle for connecting offices together. Notes enables remote locations to have up-to-date information, and can keep various parts of a business working together as a group.

What You Can Do with Lotus Notes

Lotus Notes is a very flexible product. It supports multiplatforms and networks, contains built-in multimedia capabilities, and represents a true document-management system. You can use Notes to automate workflow projects and eliminate office shuffling. You can also use Notes for tracking and discussion purposes. Other Notes applications include inventory management systems, file libraries, and management applications. Specifically, Lotus Notes has the following benefits:

Multiplatform. As a multiplatform product, your Notes network can run on Macintoshes, Windows, UNIX, and OS/2 machines at the same time while accessing the same information. Notes depends on server machines to hold and organize data, keep track of security and access privileges, share information among all the users, and route documents, files, and information.

NotesMail. Notes is also a complete e-mail package. Because e-mail is built-in, you can easily send messages to and receive messages from any other Notes user on your network. You can also send files and multimedia messages with audio and video characteristics using NotesMail.

Databases. You can use Notes for standard database applications as well. Using Notes, you can store information, discussions, files, and messages in a typical database format. Notes also allows you to import many data types and create fully customizable views to summarize and report on all the documents in your database. For example, you can easily import a Lotus 1-2-3 spreadsheet into a Notes database in order to make the data available for more uses and mail it to your colleagues.

Document routing. Because all Notes documents can be mailed to other Notes users, document routing lets you automatically send certain Notes documents using NotesMail. Notes automatically finds the mail path to any user, no matter how large your Notes network is. Some examples of document routing are exchanging your timesheets back and forth between you and your manager or sending the newest version of a program you are writing to a colleague.

Text searching and indexing. You can full-text index all Notes databases, which means that you can quickly search large amounts of data for specific items within a database. Notes can be configured to automatically re-index its databases whenever new information is added, to keep the indexes up to date. For example, if you need to search a messaging database with over 15,000 messages in it for a specific topic, the indexed database can return your desired information within a few seconds, in an easy-to-use format.

Database replication allows you to provide the same databases of information across multiple servers. If you have a database that lists all of the employees of your company, you might want that database replicated to all your servers in your Notes network. Replication allows all of the servers to have the same version of your database. If you make an update or a change to the database on any server in your Notes network, that change gets replicated throughout your whole network so that everyone can see the change. When you add an employee record to your company database, Notes automatically ensures that the record is added to all of your Notes servers with replicas of the employee database.

Workflow applications can easily be created in Notes. You use a workflow application to automatically send messages and documents to various people when certain tasks occur. For example, a simple Notes workflow application might be creating a vacation-tracking database. Associates at a company could mail in requested vacation dates to a central Notes database. Notes could automatically generate mail messages to the correct managers for vacation approval. After receiving the managers' replies, the Notes database could then send messages out to the secretarial staff about the vacation, to the payroll department so they could track vacation days, and to the associates. This type of workflow application eliminates paper shuffling and phone tag for simple, everyday activities.

Security. Lotus Notes has a strong, highly integrated security system that limits the number of people who can use your Notes networks, which databases they can access, and even which parts of the database they can read or access. Although security can become quite complex, Notes enables you to take advantage of basic security privileges to protect your data.

Basic Notes Concepts

Before you get started with this book, you should become familiar with a few basic terms. While using Notes, you will come across databases, views, forms, documents, and fields. Once you understand those terms, you should be ready to start learning how to use Notes!

In Notes, a *database* is any structure that holds information. Databases can be located on your personal computer or made widely available to everyone using the server. When you create a new database, you can customize and personalize your database to use almost any type of information. All Notes applications are built around using databases.

A *view* is the fundamental way to see information in a Notes database. Views summarize Notes documents into an easy-to-read format. You can customize views and use them to see different pieces of information in documents. You can also use views for document maintenance because they can list all available documents to update, add, or delete.

Notes databases store information in *documents*. You create Notes documents that are based on the specific fields in a form. Once documents have been created, you can list them based on certain criteria in your views.

A *form* is a customizable screen that is the basis of every document. When you create Notes documents, they are all dependent on what the form looks like. Some forms have body and date fields, and others require specific words or user names. Each database has its own forms based on what the intents of the database are. Forms can contain any combination of graphics, text, and user-entered information.

Finally, a *field* is the basic unit to store information in Notes. Placed on a form, a field is a prompt that can hold many types of information. Various types of fields are added to new forms to make them customizable for uses in Notes databases. There are special types of fields for text, dates, numbers, and rich text items (graphics and such). The columns in a database view are a summary list of fields. You can place as many unique fields as you want on a form in a Notes database.

Introduction

Task Sections

The Task sections include numbered steps that tell you how to accomplish certain tasks such as sending a message or creating a view. The numbered steps walk you through a specific example so that you can learn the task by doing it.

Big Screen

At the beginning of each task is a large screen that shows how the computer screen will look after you complete the procedure that follows in that task. Sometimes the screen shows a feature discussed in that task, however, such as a shortcut menu.

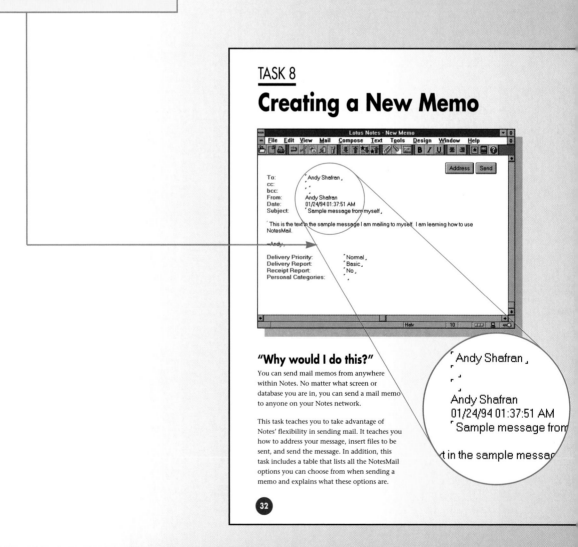

TASK 8
Creating a New Memo

"Why would I do this?"

You can send mail memos from anywhere within Notes. No matter what screen or database you are in, you can send a mail memo to anyone on your Notes network.

This task teaches you to take advantage of Notes' flexibility in sending mail. It teaches you how to address your message, insert files to be sent, and send the message. In addition, this task includes a table that lists all the NotesMail options you can choose from when sending a memo and explains what these options are.

Step-by-Step Screens

Each task includes a screen shot for each step of a procedure that shows how the computer screen will look at each step in the process.

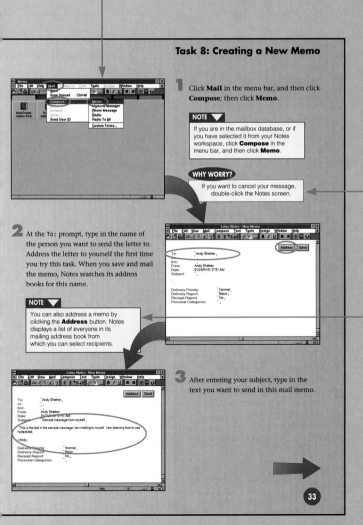

Task 8: Creating a New Memo

1 Click **Mail** in the menu bar, and then click **Compose**; then click **Memo**.

NOTE ▼

If you are in the mailbox database, or if you have selected it from your Notes workspace, click **Compose** in the menu bar, and then click **Memo**.

WHY WORRY?

If you want to cancel your message, double-click the Notes screen.

2 At the To: prompt, type in the name of the person you want to send the letter to. Address the letter to yourself the first time you try this task. When you save and mail the memo, Notes searches its address books for this name.

NOTE ▼

You can also address a memo by clicking the **Address** button. Notes displays a list of everyone in its mailing address book from which you can select recipients.

3 After entering your subject, type in the text you want to send in this mail memo.

33

Why Worry? Notes

You may find that you performed a task, such as sorting data, that you didn't want to do after all. The Why Worry notes tell you how to undo certain procedures or get out of a situation such as displaying a Help screen.

Other Notes

Many tasks contain other short notes that tell you a little more about certain procedures. These notes define terms, explain other options, refer you to other sections when applicable, and so on.

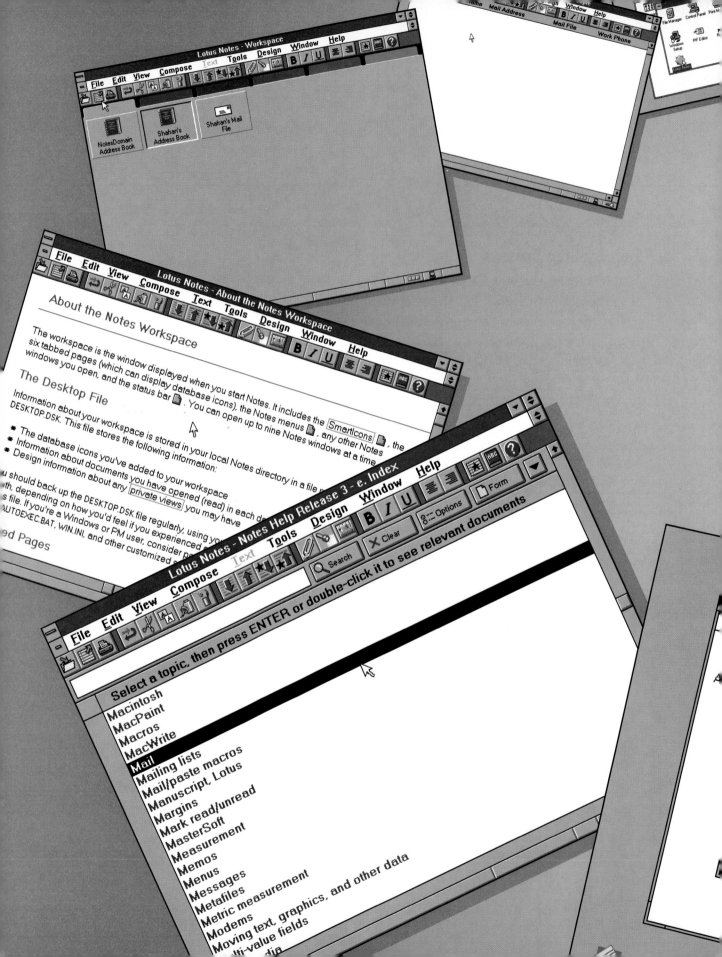

PART I

Lotus Notes Basics

In this part of the book, you learn the basics of using Lotus Notes. You learn how to start and exit Notes, how to use the mouse within Notes, and how to work with common NotesHelp functions. In addition, you learn how to access SmartIcons, and maximize, minimize, and resize the Notes window.

To access Lotus Notes, you should have the program installed on your hard disk. If you need help installing Lotus Notes onto your hard drive, see the documentation for the program. Then, you must first start Microsoft Windows. Notes should appear as a program icon in your Windows Program Manager. Once Notes is running, you can take advantage of Windows features, such as using the Clipboard and accessing a central printer.

Notes is fairly easy to use. Once you learn the basic keyboard and mouse commands, you will be able to use many Notes features with ease. Although you can perform most of the tasks with keyboard commands, you will probably prefer the mouse.

The mouse makes it easy to access the various parts of the Notes databases. With the mouse, you can select different ways to view the information in your databases (views), access and read your database entries (documents), and maneuver through the various Notes screens. A very convenient feature in Notes is the SmartIcons. *SmartIcons* are tools you activate with the mouse to perform commands, such as opening a database, sending mail, and underlining text. Because you don't have to pull down menus and select commands, SmartIcons can save you time.

Notes also contains built-in Help commands. If you would like more information about any screen or prompt within Notes, help is only a single keystroke away. The Help information answers general questions about the current screen or prompt.

In addition to the single-key Help (F1), Notes includes an indexed Help database. You can search this database for any Notes-related topic or command. The *NotesHelp index* offers thorough descriptions of almost all the features and commands in Notes. It also presents the information in a format that makes it easy to search for and locate topics. Using your mouse, you can scroll through a directory of all available topics to find the desired NotesHelp entry. In addition, you can also find the correct entries by having Notes search its NotesHelp index for full or partial text strings. The NotesHelp index is a great reference tool for learning how to access many of the intermediate and advanced features.

As in most other Windows programs, you can control and resize the Notes window. You can minimize, maximize, and resize as you like.

The tasks that follow teach you the basic skills you need to use Lotus Notes effectively.

TASK 1

Starting and Exiting Lotus Notes

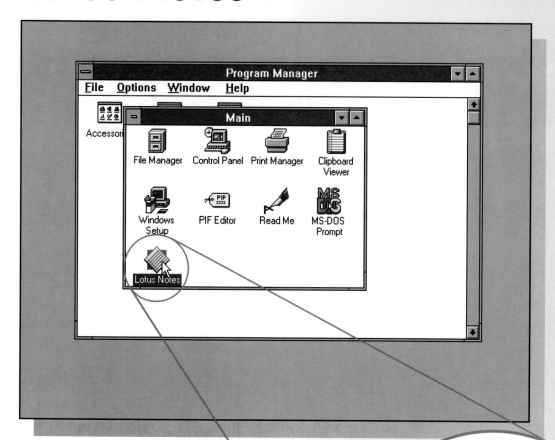

"Why would I do this?"

As with most Windows programs, you access Lotus Notes through the Windows Program Manager. During installation, Notes is placed in your Main folder on your Windows desktop.

This task shows you how to open your Main folder, and then how to open Notes. You also learn how to close and exit Notes. This task assumes that Windows is already loaded and awaiting your command.

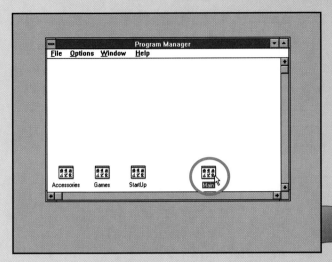

1 Search through the icons on your Windows Program Manager until you find the Main icon. Double-click the **Main** icon to open the Main folder. The folder should contain an icon labeled Lotus Notes.

2 Double-click the **Lotus Notes** icon. A green screen appears and lets you know that Notes is currently being loaded.

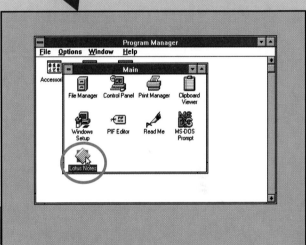

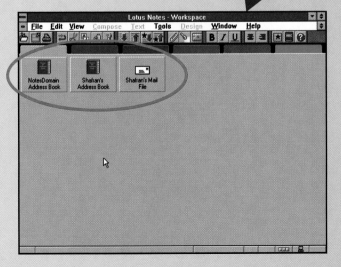

3 The Notes workspace appears on-screen. The workspace should contain a few squares similar to the ones in this example, but personalized with your name on them. You have successfully loaded Notes.

Task 1: Starting and Exiting Lotus Notes

4 To exit Notes, double-click the **Windows Control box** in the top left corner of the Notes window.

WHY WORRY?

If you have open or unsaved documents, Notes will remind you to save the documents before you exit the program.

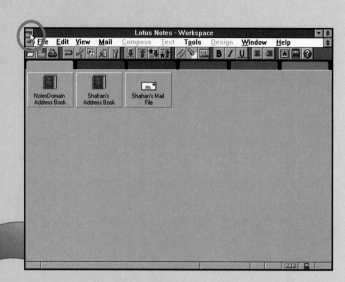

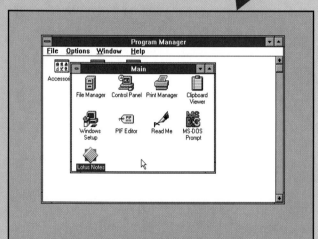

5 After successfully closing Notes, you return to Windows Program Manager where the computer awaits your next command.

NOTE ▼

You can also close Notes by clicking **File** in the menu bar and then clicking **Exit Notes**. This step chooses the File Exit command.

Using the Mouse

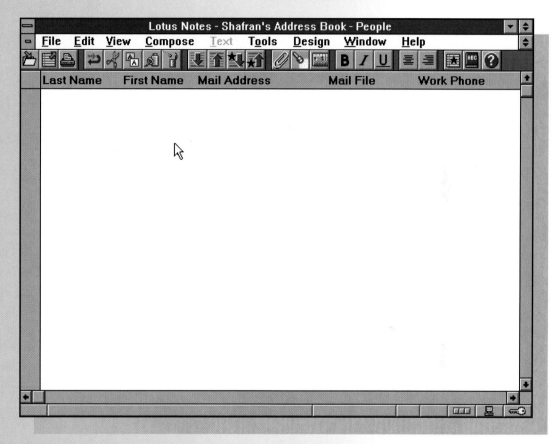

"Why would I do this?"

In Notes, the mouse has special functions. You use the mouse to navigate through the workspace, databases, and documents. You can select documents with a single mouse click. You can also open and close various screens, databases, and documents with a mere double-click.

This task shows you how to use the mouse to select, enter, and exit a database. This task assumes that you have accessed Lotus Notes from Windows Program Manager.

Task 2: Using the Mouse

1 Select your personal address book database by clicking it.

NOTE ▼

You can select multiple databases by holding down the Shift key and clicking each database in sequence.

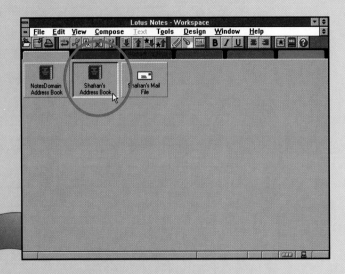

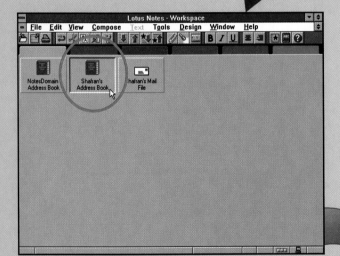

2 Open your personal address book database by placing the mouse pointer over the database and double-clicking the left mouse button. You need to open a database to read, add, change, or delete information in it.

3 To exit the database, double-click the *right* mouse button anywhere on the Notes database screen. This step closes that view, takes you out of the database, and returns you to the previous view.

NOTE ▼

To reproduce a single left click using the keyboard, press the space bar. To reproduce a double left click, press Enter. To reproduce a double right click, press Esc.

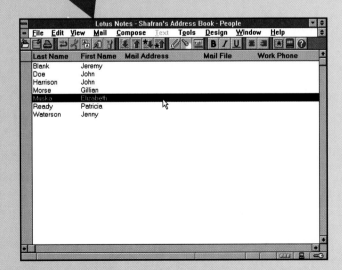

TASK 3
Using SmartIcons

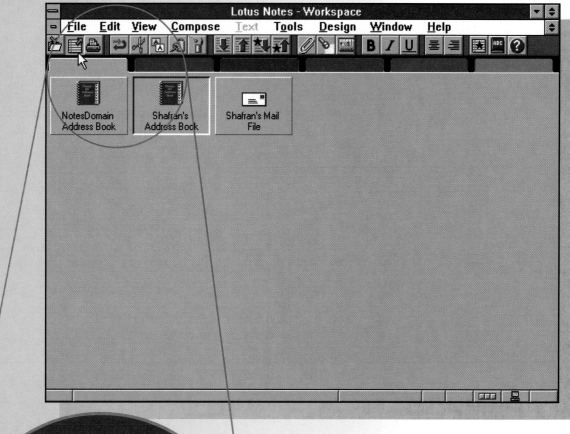

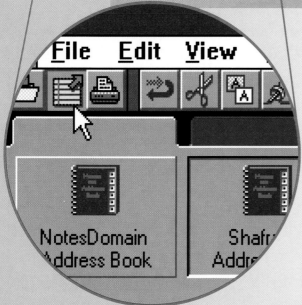

"Why would I do this?"

SmartIcons are tools you click to run various Notes commands. By default, SmartIcons are placed under the Notes menu bar. When you use a SmartIcon, you don't have to pull down a menu and choose a command—you simply click the SmartIcon. SmartIcons exist for almost all menu commands. You must use a mouse to activate SmartIcons.

This task shows you how to open a database with a SmartIcon.

Task 3: Using SmartIcons

1 Locate your address book database on the Notes workspace. Your name should appear on the database. To select it, click it.

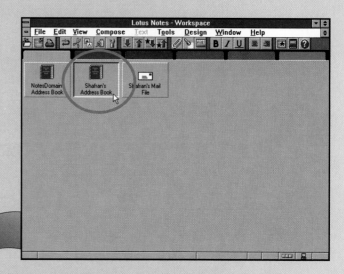

2 To open your address book database, click the **Open Database** SmartIcon.

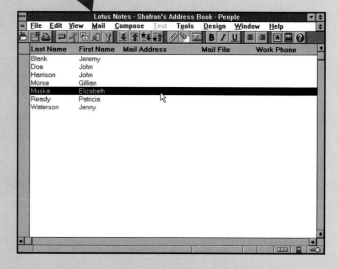

3 To exit your address book database and return to your Notes workspace, double-click with the right mouse button anywhere on the open part of the screen.

TASK 4

Using NotesHelp

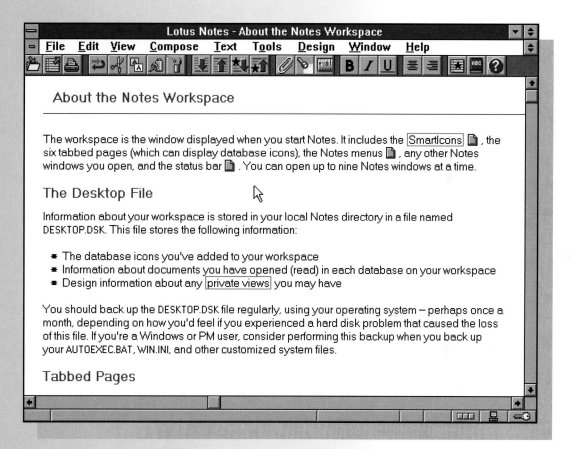

"Why would I do this?"

NotesHelp is available from any screen within Notes. If you have a question about any prompt, screen, or message, press the F1 key to display a NotesHelp screen on the item currently selected.

This task shows you how to bring up a NotesHelp screen about your Notes workspace.

Task 4: Using NotesHelp

1 Click anywhere on the gray Notes workspace to select it.

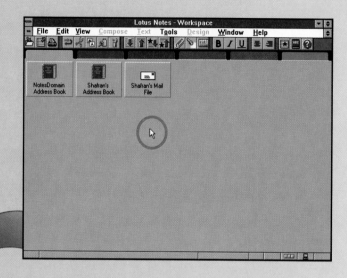

2 Press the **F1** key. This step requests help on the item you have selected—the Notes workspace. NotesHelp brings up a screen entitled About the Notes Workspace. You can scroll through this document and read about the Notes workspace.

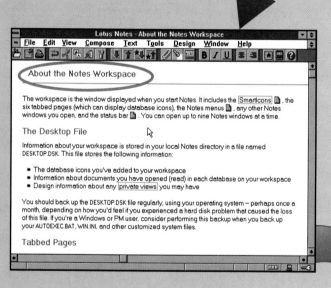

3 To access documents that are related to this topic, double-click the **small document** icon.

> **NOTE** ▼
>
> To exit NotesHelp, double-click the right mouse button anywhere on the NotesHelp screen. This step closes that page of NotesHelp and returns you to the previous screen.

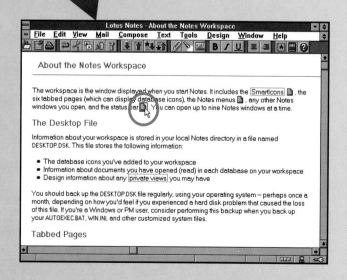

TASK 5

Using the NotesHelp Index

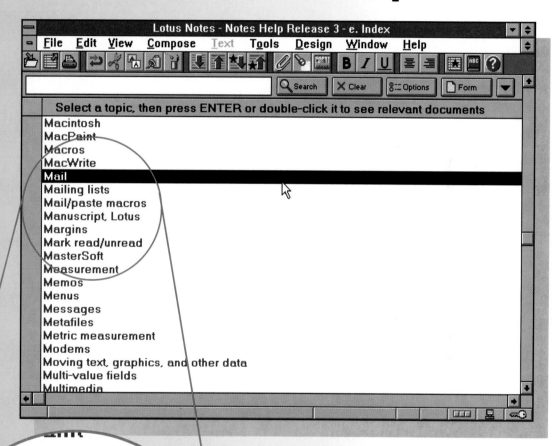

"Why would I do this?"

Another helpful feature of NotesHelp is the index. All Notes commands and options are listed in an easily accessible index. You can use the NotesHelp index to find information on such topics as opening a database, sending NotesMail, or changing your Notes password.

This task shows you how to use the index. You search for the Mail topic.

Task 5: Using the NotesHelp Index

1 Click **Help** to pull down the Help menu. Then, click **Index** to display the NotesHelp Index.

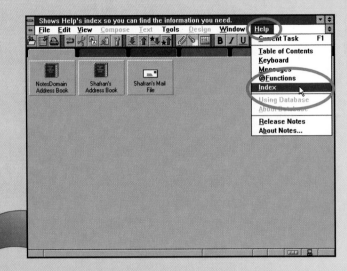

2 With the full list of Notes topics available, press the **M** key. The terms beginning with the letter M appear on-screen.

3 Click the line that contains the word *Mail* to select the mail topic.

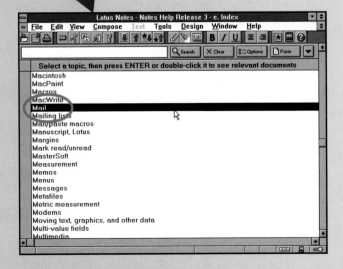

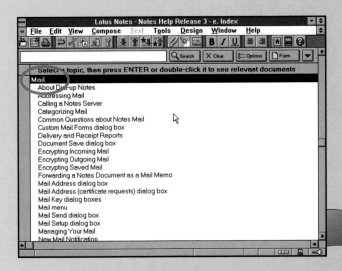

4 Double-click **Mail**. A list of subcategories appears on-screen. You can now select any one of these Mail subcategories for more information on the specific topic.

5 To exit the NotesHelp index, double-click the right mouse button anywhere on the NotesHelp screen. This step closes that screen of the NotesHelp index and returns you to the previous screen.

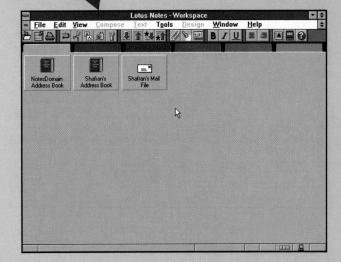

Maximizing and Minimizing the Notes Window

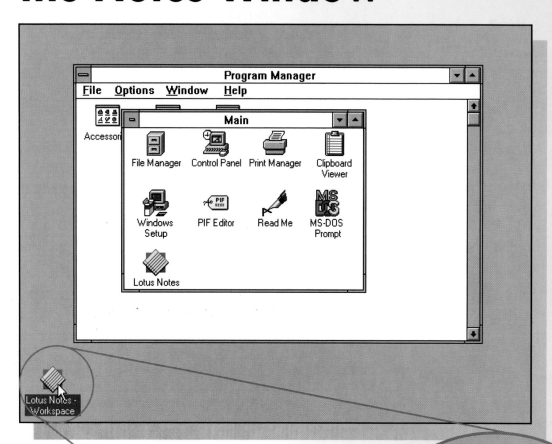

"Why would I do this?"

Similar to other Windows programs, Notes can be easily resized to fit your screen. You can maximize the Notes window, or you can minimize the Notes window so that Notes appears as a small icon on-screen. To resize the Notes window, you use the Minimize and Maximize buttons located in the upper right corner of the window.

This task shows you how to minimize and then maximize your Notes window.

Task 6: Maximizing and Minimizing the Notes Window

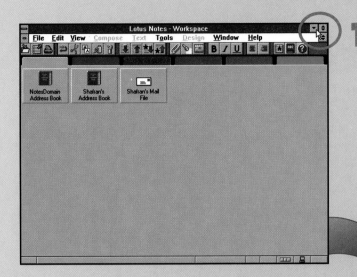

1 Locate the Minimize and Maximize buttons in the upper right corner of the Notes window. The Minimize button contains a down arrow; the Maximize button contains a down arrow and an up arrow.

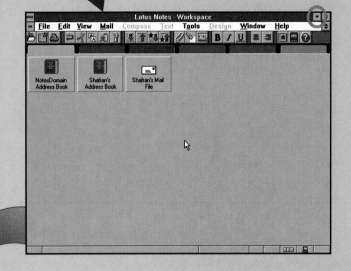

2 Click the **Minimize** button once. Notes appears as a program icon in the bottom left corner of the screen. You can perform other Windows functions while Notes is minimized.

3 To maximize Notes again, double-click the small **Notes** program icon in the lower left corner of the screen. The Notes window appears on-screen again.

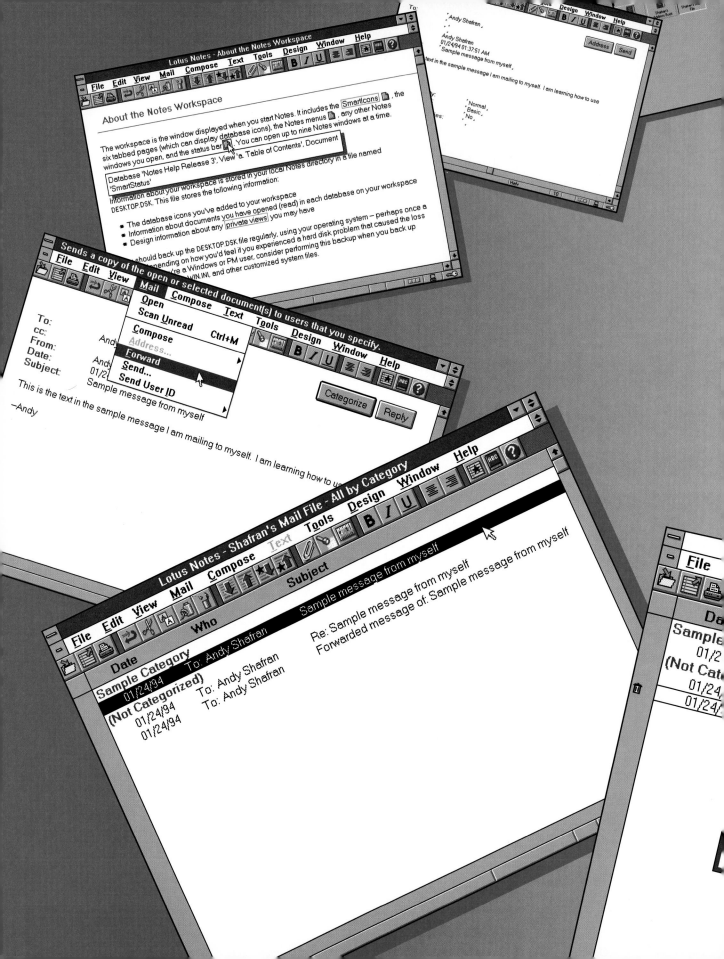

PART II
Using NotesMail

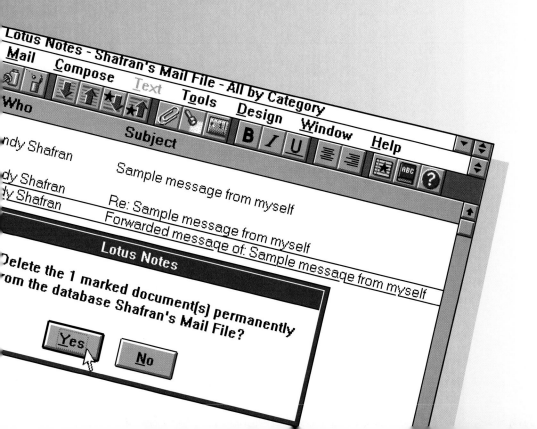

Part II: Using NotesMail

Once you are familiar with the basics of Lotus Notes, you can start taking advantage of Notes' built-in features. One of the most important built-in features is a fully functional e-mail system called NotesMail. Advanced features such as document sharing, message routing, and mail forwarding rely on some NotesMail basics in order to operate.

This part teaches you these basics and explains how to use some special mail options and commands. You learn how to open your personal mailbox database and read your messages.

Your Notes mailbox is a unique database on your workspace. Only you can access it. Many views are included with your mailbox to make it easier to sort the mail you have received and reference it later. You can sort your incoming and outgoing mail by size, date, sender, and category.

A later section teaches you how to create a message from top to bottom. The Create Message task covers addressing, entering your text, and mailing your message. You learn how to send, save, sign, encrypt, address, and prioritize your messages, as well as how to use message receipts. In addition to sending text to other users, you can also send files. Notes lets you include as many files as you want in a mail message.

Built into sending and receiving NotesMail is replying to received messages. Composing a reply message to any message in your personal mailbox database is a simple task.

In Notes, the documents in all databases are mail-enabled, which means you can forward any document in any database to another user using NotesMail. It takes only one menu command to create a memo message with the document enclosed inside. When you forward a document, a regular memo message appears on-screen with the forwarded message in the memo text body field. You can address it to the recipient(s) of your choice, categorize it for personal use, and treat it as any other NotesMail message.

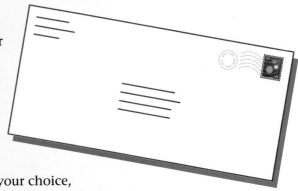

When you start getting a lot of mail, you need to know how to keep your mailbox database in order. You can organize your mailbox by categorizing mail or deleting unnecessary letters. Categorizing your messages makes it easy for you to find information and messages for future reference and is as simple as a few mouse clicks.

Lotus Notes has built-in verification of deletion, which prevents you from accidentally deleting messages. Whenever you select a message for deletion, Notes verifies that request by prompting you for your authorization before deleting the message.

Reading NotesMail

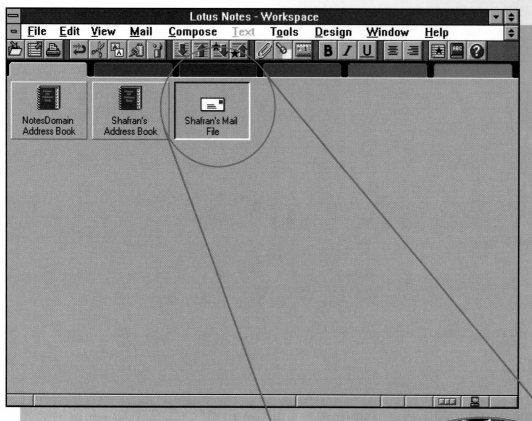

"Why would I do this?"

Although you can compose and send mail messages when you are not in your mailbox database, you must be in your mailbox database to read, edit, and sort your personal mail messages because all your mail is sent there. This setup makes it easier to keep track of your mail because it's all in one central location.

This task shows you the most direct way to access your mailbox database from any screen in Lotus Notes.

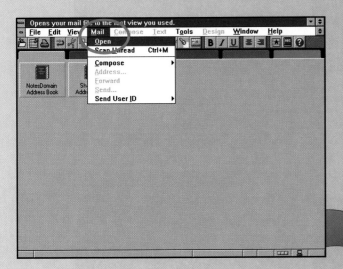

1 Click **Mail** on the menu bar at the top of the screen, and then click **Open**.

NOTE ▼

You can also open your mailbox directly from your workspace by double-clicking your mailbox database. Your mailbox database is personalized and has a letter icon identifying it.

2 All the messages in your mailbox are listed on-screen. To read a message, double-click it. The message opens.

NOTE ▼

If you are a new Notes user, you might not have any messages waiting for you.

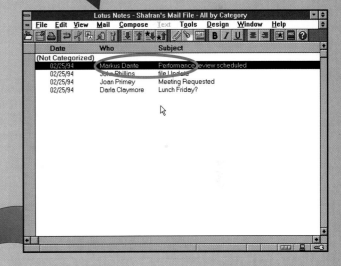

3 To return to your Notes workspace, double-click your screen to exit your current message, and then double-click again to exit your mailbox database.

Creating a New Memo

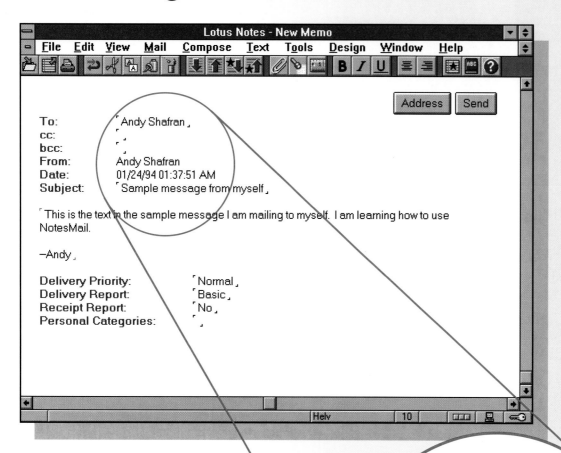

"Why would I do this?"

You can send mail memos from anywhere within Notes. No matter what screen or database you are in, you can send a mail memo to anyone on your Notes network.

This task teaches you to take advantage of Notes' flexibility in sending mail. It teaches you how to address your message, insert files to be sent, and send the message. In addition, this task includes a table that lists all the NotesMail options you can choose from when sending a memo and explains what these options are.

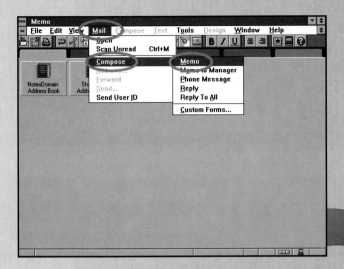

1 Click **Mail** in the menu bar, and then click **Compose**; then click **Memo**.

NOTE ▼

If you are in the mailbox database, or if you have selected it from your Notes workspace, click **Compose** in the menu bar, and then click **Memo**.

WHY WORRY?

If you want to cancel your message, double-click the Notes screen.

2 At the To: prompt, type in the name of the person you want to send the letter to. Address the letter to yourself the first time you try this task. When you save and mail the memo, Notes searches its address books for this name.

NOTE ▼

You can also address a memo by clicking the **Address** button. Notes displays a list of everyone in its mailing address book from which you can select recipients.

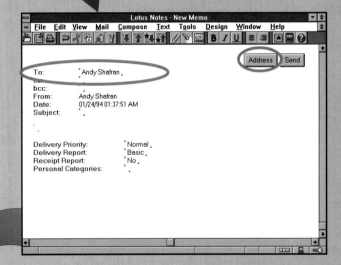

3 After entering your subject, type in the text you want to send in this mail memo.

Task 8: Creating a New Memo

4 To send a file with your mail memo, click **File** on the Notes menu bar; then click **Attach** to display an Insert Attachments window.

5 Scan through your hard drive until you have located the file you want to attach. Select that file by clicking it.

6 Click the **Insert** button to insert the selected file into your mail memo.

NOTE ▼

You can also include graphics pasted in from the Windows Clipboard in your mail memos.

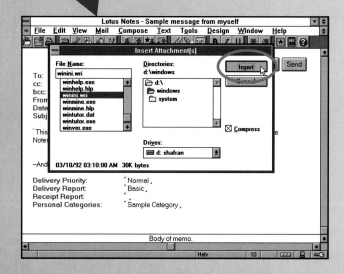

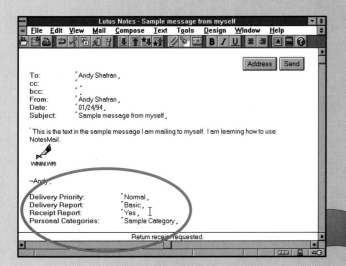

7 To specify delivery options, fill in the prompts at the bottom of the memo. `Priority` controls how fast your network delivers the memo. Enter C at the `Delivery Report` prompt to have Notes notify you when the memo is delivered. Enter Y at the `Receipt Report` prompt to have Notes notify you when your memo recipients have read the memo.

`Personal Categories` sorts saved memos into one of your personal categories.

8 To send your letter, double-click the Notes workspace with the right mouse button to display the Document Save dialog box. Select the options you want (the following table explains these); then click **Yes** to send your mail.

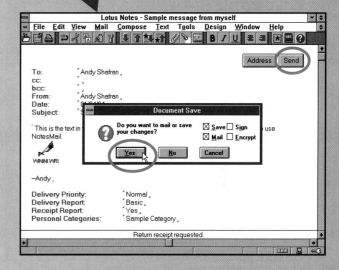

NOTE ▼

You can also click the **Send** button to send your message.

Send Option	Description
Mail	Ensures that Notes sends a copy of your memo to each of your recipients.
Save	Tells Notes to save a copy of the outgoing memo in your mailbox database.
Sign	Verifies whether your mail has been viewed or tampered with during the delivery process.
Encrypt	Makes a message readable to the recipient only.

Replying to a Memo

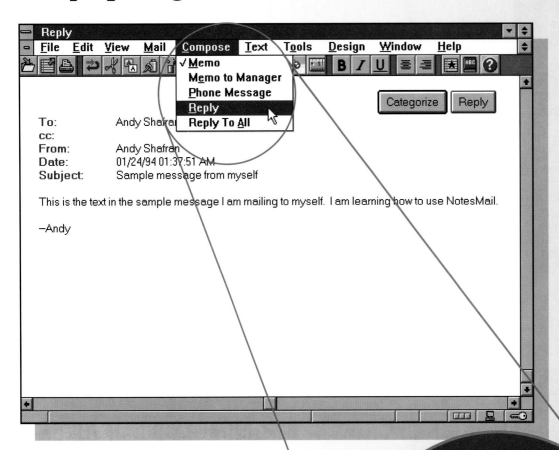

"Why would I do this?"

Often you will want to respond to someone who has sent you NotesMail messages. This task shows you how to create and send a reply message to a received NotesMail memo. Instead of creating a whole new memo, you use the Lotus Notes' Reply command to address the message and fill in the Subject: prompt for you.

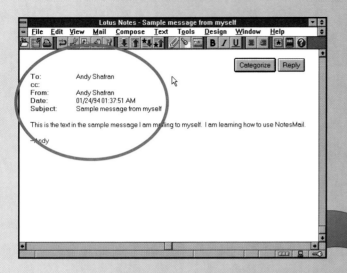

1 Using your mouse, double-click the message you want to reply to (you must first be in your personal mailbox database).

2 Click **Compose** in the menu bar, and then click **Reply** to display a reply message form.

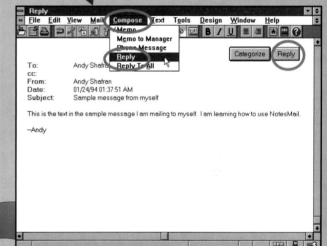

> **NOTE** ▼
>
> You can also click the **Reply** button to display the reply form.

3 Add additional addresses, type in your message, save the reply message, and send it like a regular mail message.

Forwarding a Document

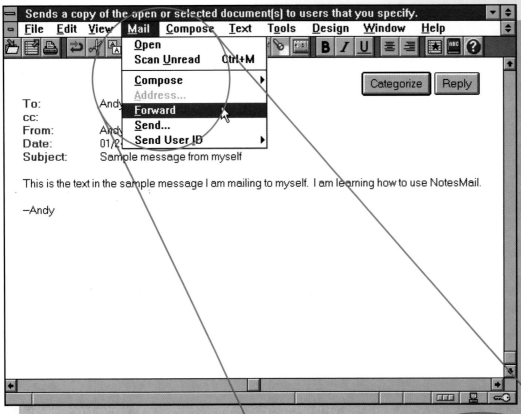

"Why would I do this?"

If you are reading a database, and come across a document you want to send to someone else, you can use Notes' built-in forwarding feature. You can forward any message in any database to another Notes user.

This task describes how to forward a document by adding it to a memo message and then sending it to another user.

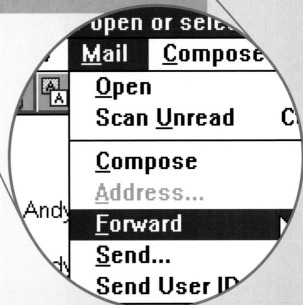

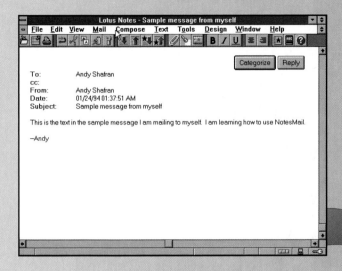

1 Ensure that you are reading or highlighting the message you want to forward to another user.

2 Click **Mail** from the menu bar, and then click **Forward** to display a memo message form.

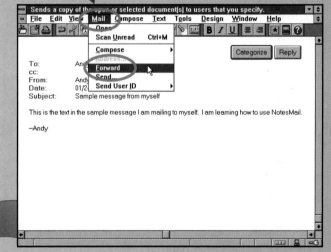

3 Address the memo, type in your message, save the memo, and send it like a regular mail message.

Sorting and Categorizing Your NotesMail

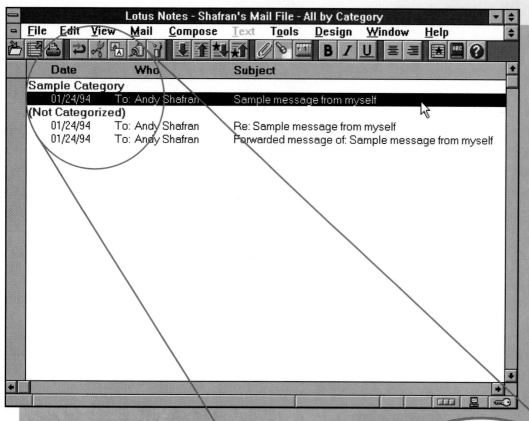

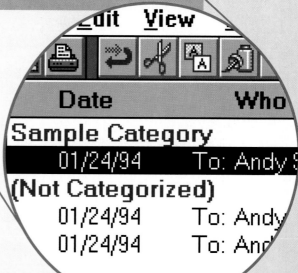

"Why would I do this?"

After awhile, you may start to accumulate many mail messages in your personal mailbox data-base. Although you can delete those you no longer need, you may want to save some messages for future reference. You can categorize and sort any mail message in your mailbox under one or more category heading(s).

This task shows you how to add a new category and sort a message in your personal mailbox database.

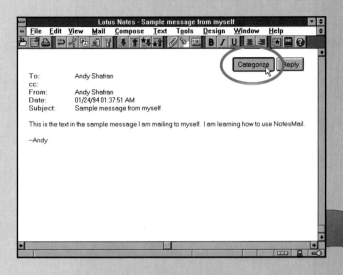

1 While reading the message you want to categorize, click the **Categorize** button to display the Categorize dialog box.

2 Click the New Categories text box and type **Sample Category**. Click the **OK** button to categorize your message.

> **NOTE** ▼
>
> The Categorize dialog box lists the available categories. (In the example, no categories are available.) To choose one of these categories instead of creating a new one, just double-click the one you want.

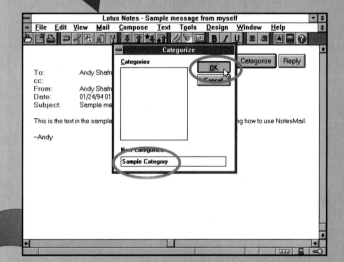

3 Scan through your personal mailbox database to ensure that your message is now sorted by the Sample Category.

TASK 12
Deleting Mail

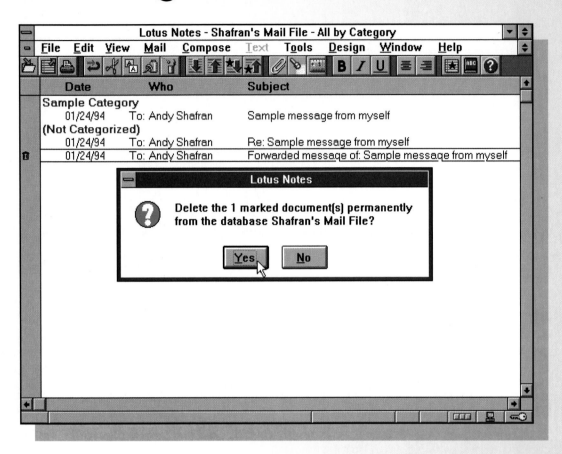

"Why would I do this?"

Soon you will start accumulating many mail messages in your personal mailbox database. Although you may want to save or categorize some of those messages for future use, you will probably be able to delete most of them. This task explains how to do this.

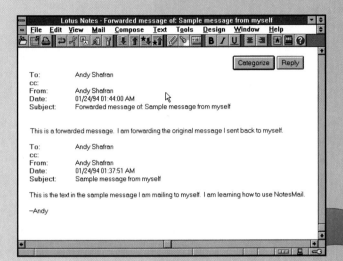

1 While reading or highlighting the message you want to delete, press the **Delete** key on your keyboard to mark it for deletion.

NOTE ▼

You can also select and delete multiple messages simultaneously. Select all the messages you want to delete with your mouse button and then press the **Delete** key.

2 Notes returns you to mailbox view. Note that the message you marked for deletion in the preceding step has a miniature trash can next to it.

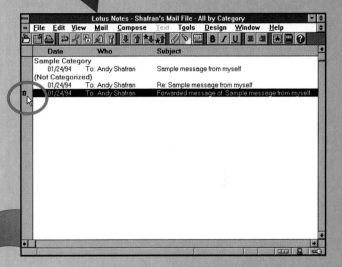

3 Press **F9** (the Refresh key). Notes asks you whether you really want to delete the messages you marked. Click **Yes** to verify deletion.

WHY WORRY?

If you exit the mailbox database or Notes before hitting the **F9** key, Notes prompts you to make sure you really want to delete those messages marked for deletion.

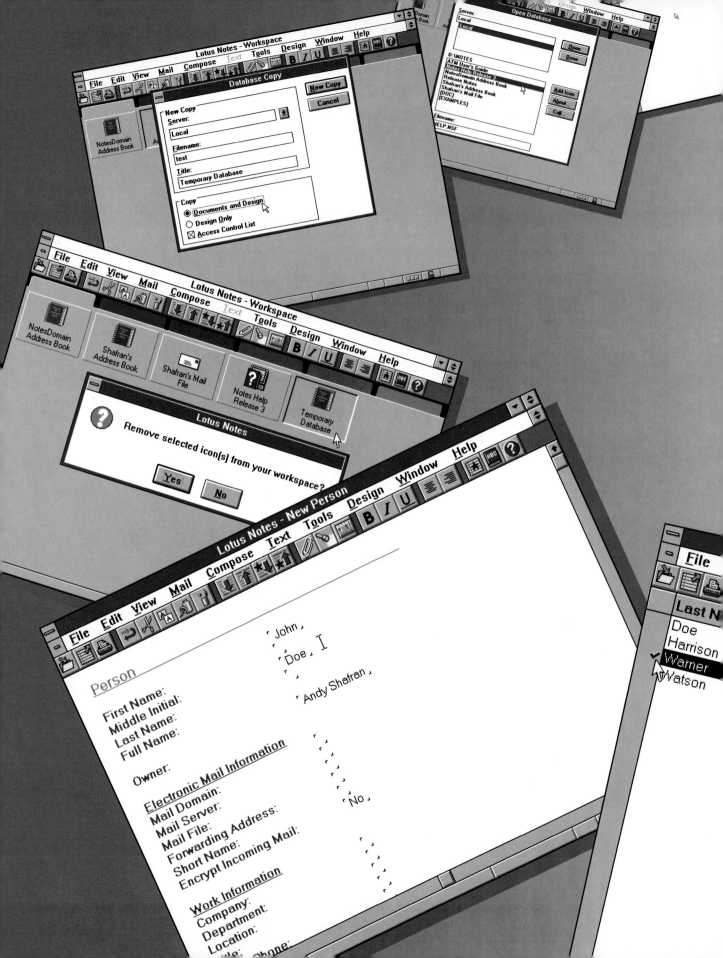

PART III

Accessing and Using Notes Databases

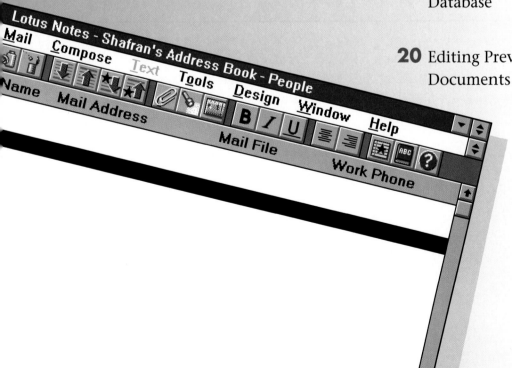

Part III: Accessing and Using Notes Databases

L otus Notes is built primarily of various databases. Whether you use a mailbox database or a project development system, every database is dependent on Notes' consistent database structure. Certain commands work on all databases in Notes no matter what their purpose. You can open, close, copy, remove, and add all databases on your workspace in the same way. This consistency makes it easy to share databases and Notes applications between groups and departments because everyone can access them the same way. However, each database has its own unique characteristics as well.

Each database has its own set of documents you can compose and views to see that information. For example, an address book database may have different documents for businesses, government locations, and people. That database may have a separate view set up for each document type and one special combined view that lists all addresses regardless of type. Another example might be a a project management database. This application may have separate documents to work on the project, to review the status, to get management approval, and to ask questions about the project. There may be a special view set up for managers only to view all management approval situations and a general view for everyone to look at questions concerning the project.

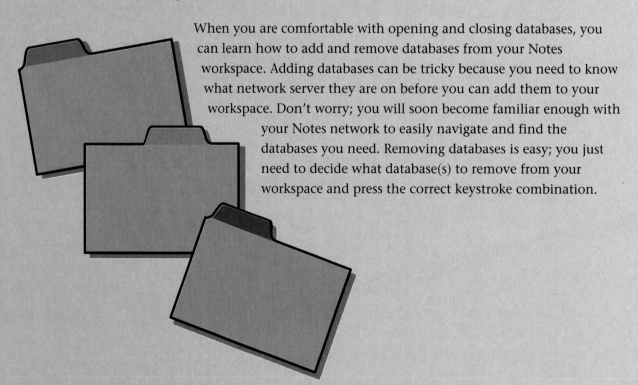

When you are comfortable with opening and closing databases, you can learn how to add and remove databases from your Notes workspace. Adding databases can be tricky because you need to know what network server they are on before you can add them to your workspace. Don't worry; you will soon become familiar enough with your Notes network to easily navigate and find the databases you need. Removing databases is easy; you just need to decide what database(s) to remove from your workspace and press the correct keystroke combination.

The last database command you learn in this part is copying a database. You will need to copy databases for backup, security, and ease of use purposes. You should always have backup copies of all important databases in case something goes wrong with Notes or your network. Sometimes you do not want some information available on your network. You could create a local copy of the database and make your changes there instead of putting the information in a public database. Copying a database involves a simple combination of steps that require you to name and/or relocate the new databases.

Once you enter any database, you should become familiar with the documents you can compose and the views you can access. Composing a document is as simple as choosing a command from the menu bar in Notes and entering the information required for that particular document. Each database has different forms available under the Compose menu heading. Using views is just as easy as composing documents. You can access all the previously created views under the View command from the menu bar. Just like documents that you can compose, views are different for each database as well.

After you master database maintenance commands and the Compose and View sections of databases, you will understand how to access most of the commands in all databases in Lotus Notes.

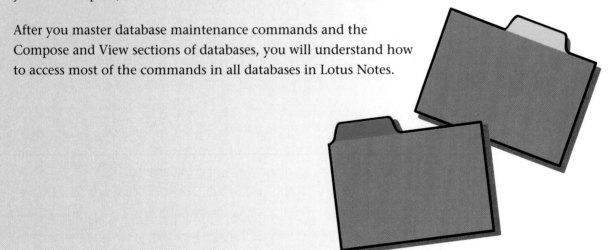

TASK 13

Opening and Closing a Database

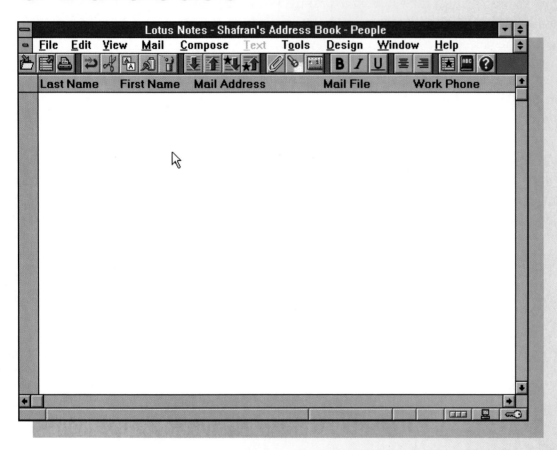

"Why would I do this?"

Before you can learn how to add, remove, and copy databases, you must learn how to access them. Opening and closing databases are two of the most basic and common activities in Notes.

This task will teach you how to open and close your personal address book database.

48

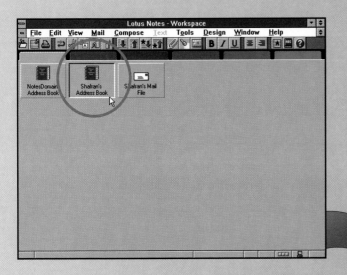

1 Select your personal address book database by clicking it.

2 Open your personal address book database by placing the mouse pointer over the database and double-clicking. The default view appears and shows the documents that are in your database.

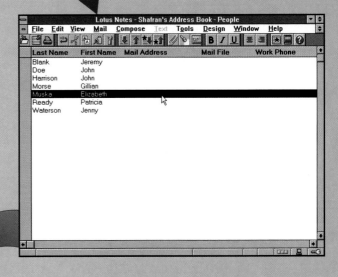

3 To close the database, double-click with your *right* mouse button anywhere on the Notes database screen. This action closes the view, exits the database, and returns you to the Notes workspace.

Adding a New Database to Your Workspace

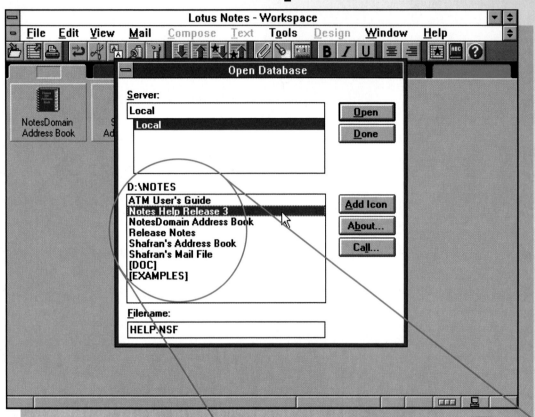

"Why would I do this?"

When Notes is first installed, a default set of databases is placed on your workspace. This default set usually includes a company address book, your personal mailbox, and your personal address book. Adding new databases is very easy to do.

This task shows you how to add a new database to your Notes workspace.

D:\NOTES

ATM User's Guide
Notes Help Release 3
NotesDomain Address Boo
Release Notes
Shafran's Address Book
Shafran's Mail File
[DOC]
[EXAMPLES]

Task 14: Adding a New Database to Your Workspace

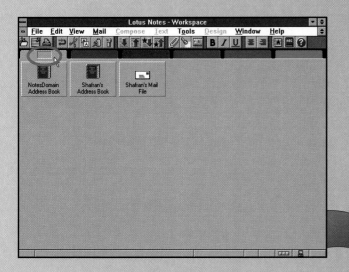

1 Ensure that you are on the correct file folder page by using your mouse to navigate between pages. The database will be added to the current page.

2 Click **File** from the menu bar, and then click **Open Database** to display the Open Database dialog box,

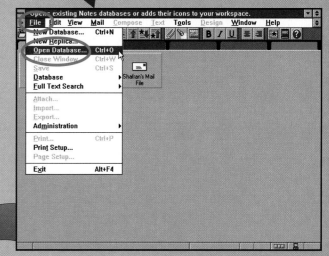

3 Scroll through the list of servers available until you locate **Local**. Double-click **Local** to display a list of available databases.

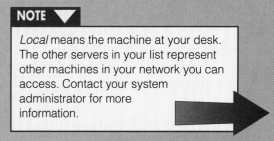

> ### NOTE ▼
>
> *Local* means the machine at your desk. The other servers in your list represent other machines in your network you can access. Contact your system administrator for more information.

Task 14: Adding a New Database to Your Workspace

4 Scroll through the list of databases and select the one you want to add to your Notes workspace by clicking it.

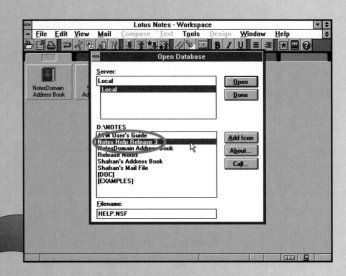

5 Click the **Add Icon** button to add the new database to your workspace.

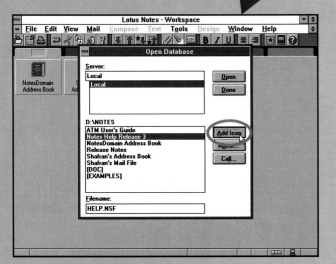

> **NOTE** ▼
>
> You can also double-click the database to have Notes automatically add the database to your workspace and open it for you.

Copying a Database to Your Local Machine

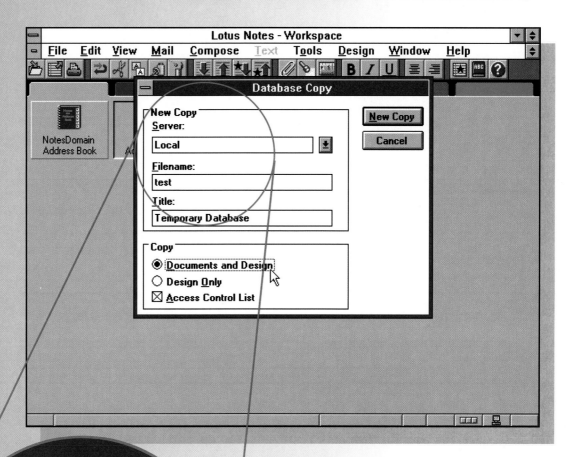

"Why would I do this?"

You should make copies of your databases from time to time in order to have a backup in case the network or Notes shuts down. Copying also comes in handy when you're designing databases.

This task shows you how to make a local copy of your personal address book. It also explains the copy options and explains how to change the title of the database copy.

Task 15: Copying a Database to Your Local Machine

1 Select your personal address book database by clicking it.

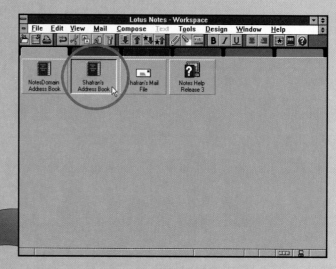

2 Click **File** on the menu bar, and then click **Database**. Click **Copy** to display the Database Copy dialog box.

3 Select the location where you want to place the new copy from the Server list box. For now, leave the word **Local** in that box so the copy is placed on your machine at your desk.

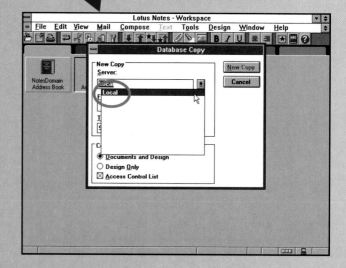

Task 15: Copying a Database to Your Local Machine

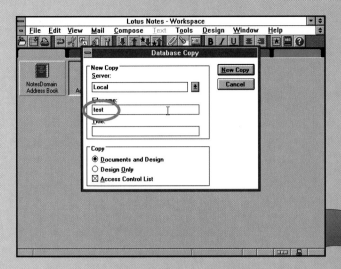

4 Enter a new file name for the copy in the Filename text box. The database file name can be a maximum of eight characters long. For this copy, enter **test**.

5 Enter a title for the database in the Title text box. For this copy, enter **Temporary Database**. The title appears with the database icon on your Notes workspace.

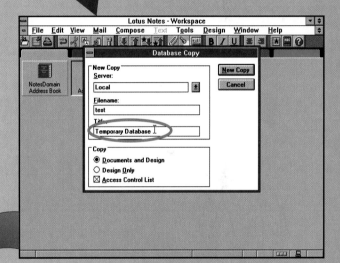

> **NOTE** ▼
>
> Documents and Design tells Notes to copy all the documents and structure from the original database. Design Only tells Notes to copy only the structure of the original database, not the documents. Access Control List tells Notes to keep the same access list on the database copy.

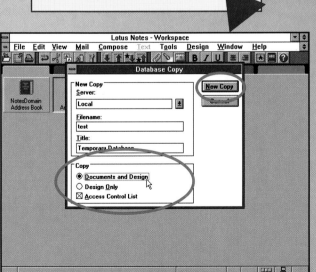

6 Click the **Documents and Design** option button to select it and click the **Access Control List** check box to deselect it. Then click the **New Copy** button to copy the database.

TASK 16

Removing a Database from Your Workspace

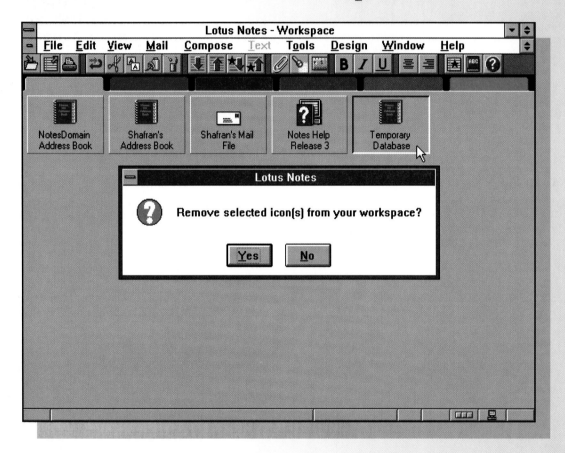

"Why would I do this?"

When you start to accumulate databases on your Notes workspace, you may need to remove one to clear some space. When you remove a database from your workspace, you are not deleting it or affecting it in any way. You are simply removing its icon from a file folder. You can always add the database if you need it again by following the steps in the previous task. This task shows you how to remove a database from one of the file folders on your workspace.

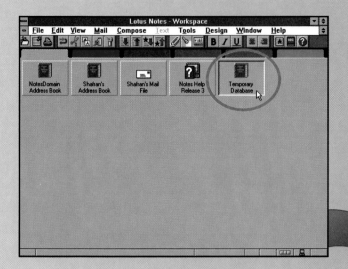

1 Click the **Temporary Database** icon to select the database you just created.

NOTE ▼

Press the Shift key while selecting databases with your mouse to mark multiple databases for removal.

2 Press the **Delete** key to display a Notes prompt box verifying database removal. This procedure removes the database from your workspace, but does not actually delete the database.

NOTE ▼

Choosing **Clear** from the **Edit** menu also displays the removal verification box.

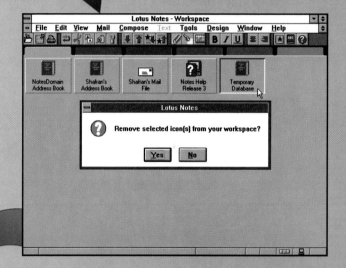

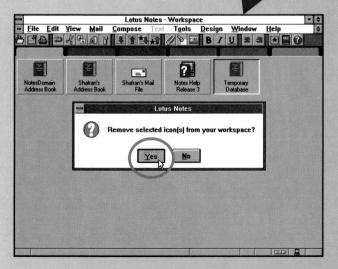

3 Click the **Yes** button to remove the database from your workspace.

TASK 17

Composing Documents in a Database

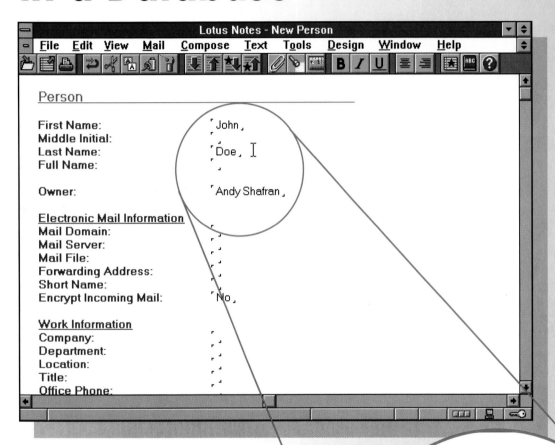

"Why would I do this?"

Each database has its own unique document types that require different types of information. This task shows you how to create a Person document in your personal address book. A Person document is a document that stores basic information about your acquaintances. This task creates a document and enters a little information about a fictitious person.

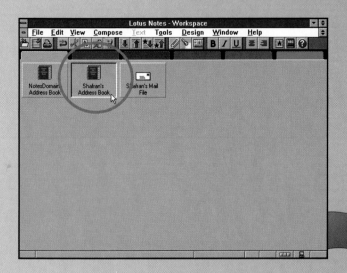

1 Open your personal address book database by placing the mouse pointer over the database icon and double-clicking.

> **NOTE** ▼
>
> You can also compose new documents from the Notes workspace if the database is selected.

2 Click **Compose** on the menu bar, and then click **Person** to display a Person form.

> **NOTE** ▼
>
> Every document has a form associated with it. The form has fields for all the information you need to create a specific type of document.

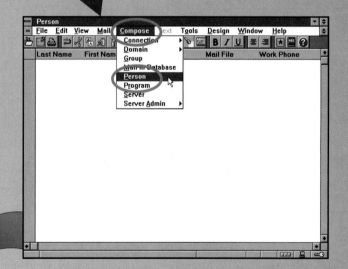

3 Enter a sample first and last name (**John Doe**, in this example) in their respective fields on the empty Person form.

Task 17: Composing Documents in a Database

4 Click **File** on the menu bar and then click **Save** to save the information as a Person document.

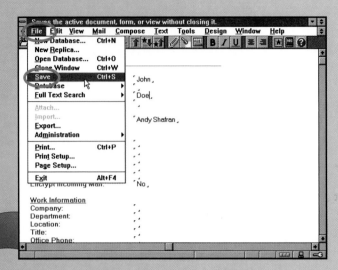

5 Double-click with your *right* mouse button to exit the database and return to the Address Book view. Your new entry (John Doe) should now be listed in the database.

6 Repeat steps 1 through 5 three additional times, creating Person documents for Jenny Watson, John Harrison, and Deb Warner (for use in future tasks).

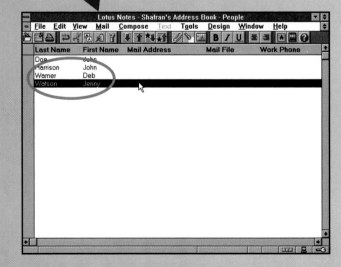

Selecting a Document

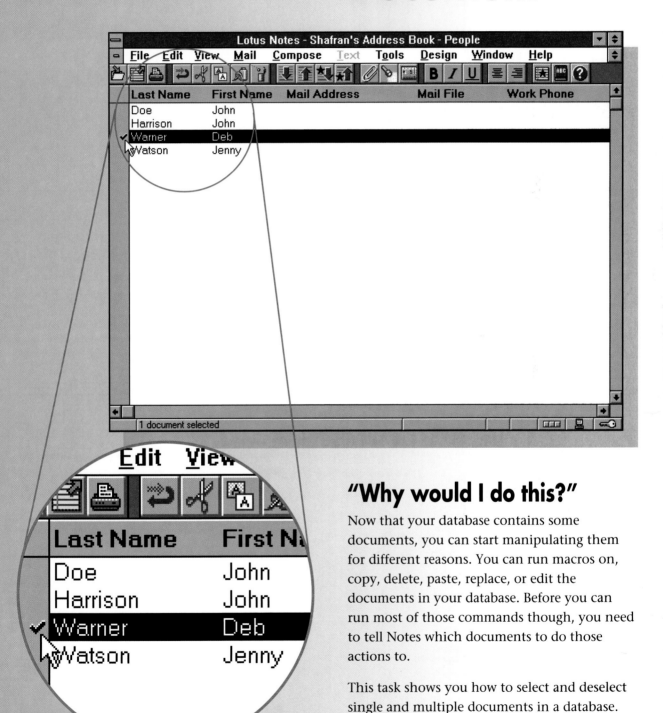

"Why would I do this?"

Now that your database contains some documents, you can start manipulating them for different reasons. You can run macros on, copy, delete, paste, replace, or edit the documents in your database. Before you can run most of those commands though, you need to tell Notes which documents to do those actions to.

This task shows you how to select and deselect single and multiple documents in a database.

Task 18: Selecting a Document

1 Ensure that you are in your personal address book database by placing the mouse pointer over the database and double-clicking.

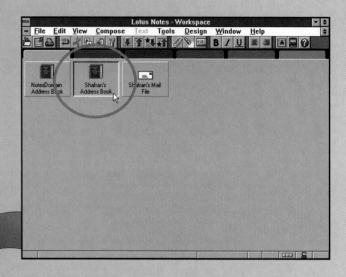

2 Select the Deb Warner document by clicking the gray space to the left of the document. A check mark should appear.

> **NOTE** ▼
>
> You can also use the arrow keys to manipulate the cursor in the view and use the space bar to select the document.

3 To deselect the document, repeat step 2 to remove the little check mark.

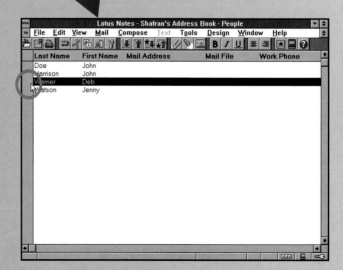

TASK 19

Deleting Documents from a Database

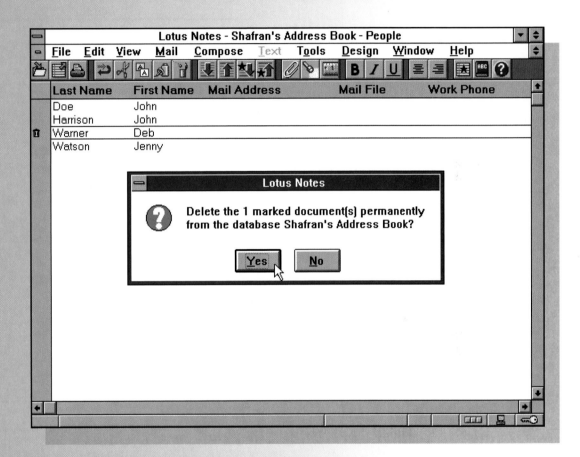

"Why would I do this?"

Sometime soon, you will need to be able to delete documents out of your database. Whether a document has become out-of-date or there are too many documents in your database, you need to know how to get rid of them.

This task shows you how to delete documents that you no longer need. You can delete one or multiple documents at a time.

Task 19: Deleting Documents from a Database

1 While in your personal address book database, highlight the document you want to delete by clicking anywhere on that line. Highlight the line with Deb Warner on it.

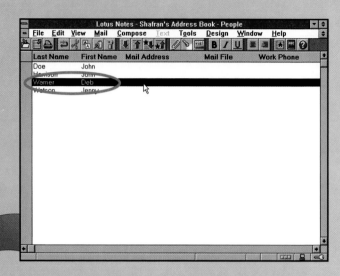

2 Press the **Delete** key to mark the document for deletion. A miniature trash can appears in the margin to the left of the document.

> **NOTE** ▼
>
> You can select as many documents as you want for deletion at one time.

3 Press the **F9** (refresh) key to update the screen and verify the deletion by clicking the **Yes** button.

> **WHY WORRY?**
>
> In case you accidentally mark the wrong document for deletion and hit the F9 key, Notes automatically asks you for verification before it permanently deletes the document.

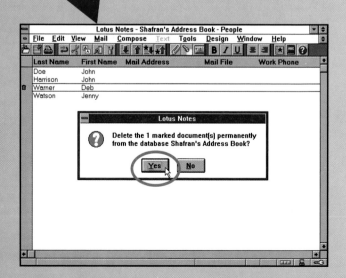

Editing Previously Created Documents

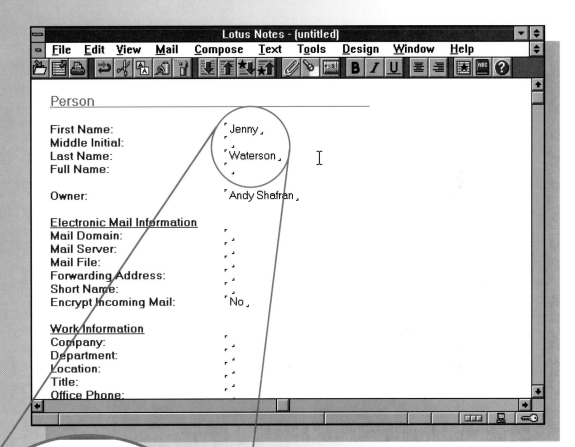

"Why would I do this?"

Sometimes you may need to make updates in documents that are already created. For example, if a client moved and you need to change her address, or if you accidentally mistyped a name, you need to go in and edit that particular document.

This task shows you how to edit an existing document. You change the last name of one of the Person documents you created in a previous task.

Task 20: Editing Previously Created Documents

1 Ensure that you are in the document that you want to make changes to. For this task, make sure you are reading the Jenny Watson Person document.

NOTE

You can also edit a document from a view. Highlight the document you want to edit by clicking it.

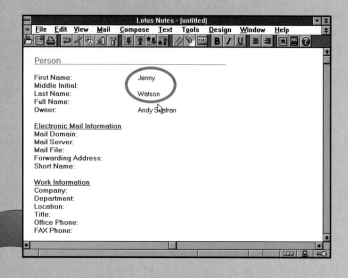

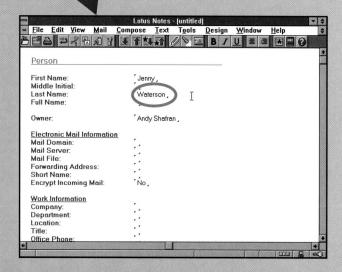

2 Click **Edit** from the menu bar and then click **Edit Document** to change Notes into edit mode.

3 Change the last name from Watson to **Waterson** by typing in the Last Name field.

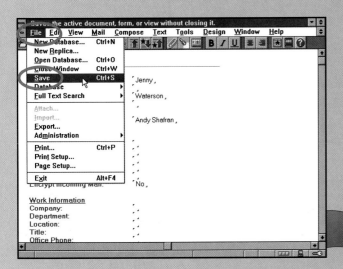

4 Click **File** on the menu bar, and then click **Save** to save the changes made to the document.

5 Click **Edit** on the menu bar, and then click **Edit Document** to change Notes into read-only mode.

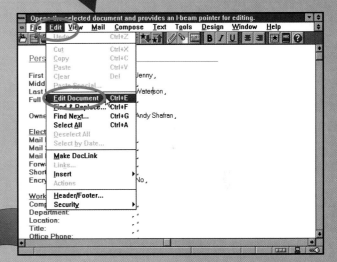

6 On your Notes workspace, double-click with your *right* mouse button to return to the view. Notice the changes that have occurred.

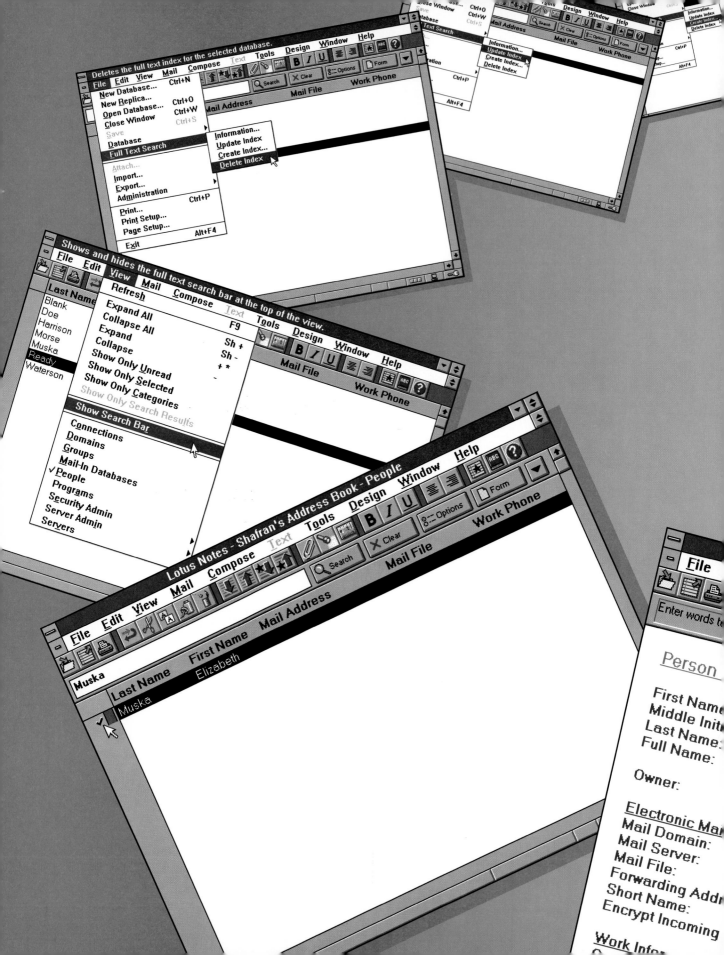

PART IV

Using the Full Text Search Commands

Creating a Full Text Index

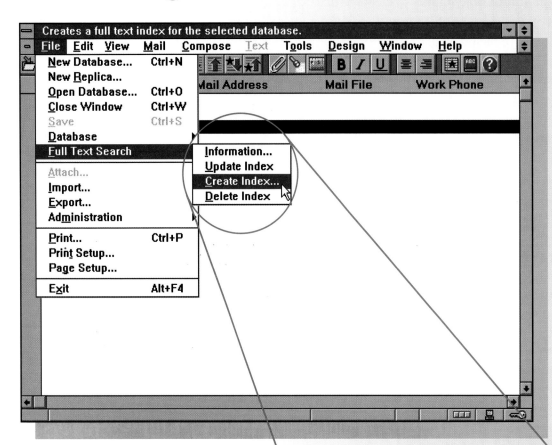

"Why would I do this?"

Before you can use Notes to search your databases, you must first create a full text index. Once you create the index, you can search for specific pieces of information.

This task takes you through the steps for creating a full text index.

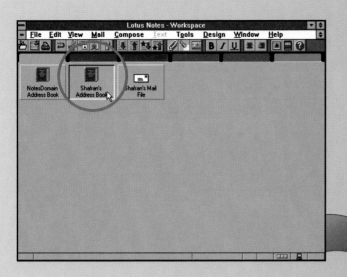

1 Highlight or open the database for which you want to create a full text index by clicking the database icon on your workspace.

2 Click **File** on the menu bar, and then click **Full Text Search**. Finally, click **Create Index**. The Full Text Create Index dialog box appears.

NOTE ▼

To learn about the create index options, press the **F1** key.

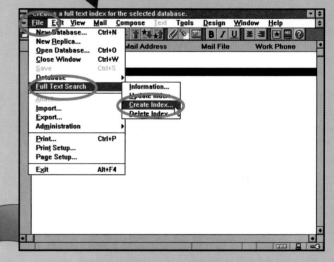

3 Click the **OK** button to create a full text index with the default options.

WHY WORRY?

If you select the incorrect options, you can always re-create the full text index with the new options overwriting the previous ones.

Task 21: Creating a Full Text Index

4 In the dialog box that appears, click the
Yes button to create the full text index for
that database.

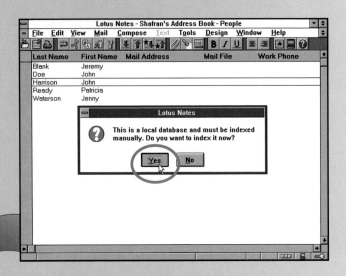

5 After Notes presents the results from the
full text index, click the **OK** button to
finish the index creation.

> **NOTE** ▼
>
> Notes adds a search bar underneath the
> row of SmartIcons to indicate the com-
> pletion of the index creation process.

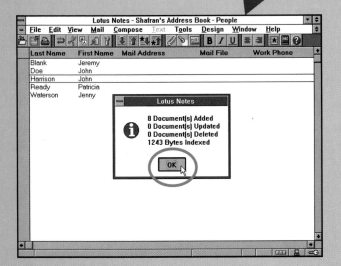

Updating a Full Text Index

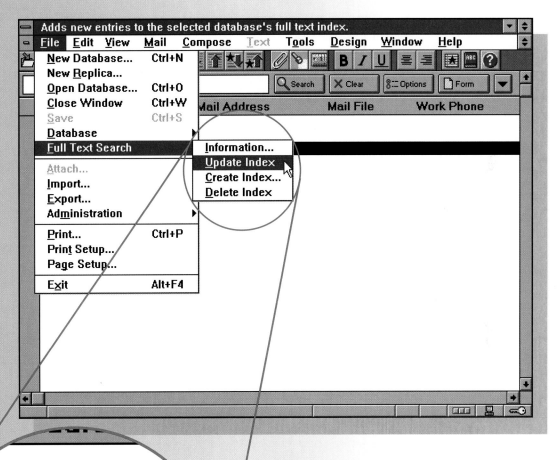

"Why would I do this?"

When you create a full text index on a database that resides on your hard drive, Notes does not automatically update the index when new documents are added to that database. An out-of-date index may result in recently added documents not showing up as results of a search. To ensure that your full text index is current, you must update it on a regular basis.

Task 22: Updating a Full Text Index

1 Highlight or open the database for which you want to update a full text index by clicking the database icon on your workspace.

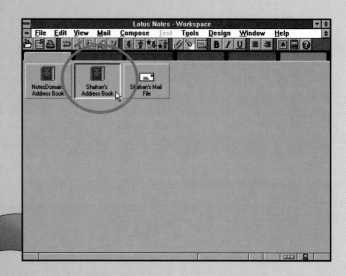

2 Click **File** on the menu bar, and then click **Full Text Search**. Then click **Update Index**.

3 In the dialog box that appears, click the **OK** button to finish the index update. If there are no new documents in your database, Notes informs you of that fact and cancels the update process.

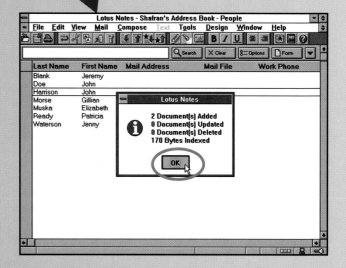

Deleting a Full Text Index

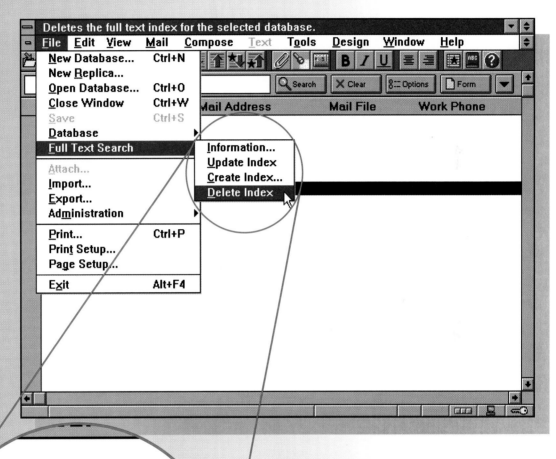

"Why would I do this?"

If there is too much information in a database to be efficiently indexed, a full text index may become quite large and slow down other database processes considerably. Sometimes a database may be used quite often, but its search functions are never accessed. To free up space and Notes resources, you may want to delete a full text index associated with a database.

Task 23: Deleting a Full Text Index

1 Highlight or open the database for which you want to delete a full text index by clicking the database icon on your workspace.

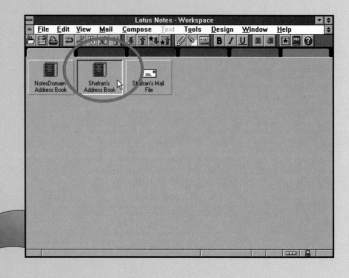

2 Click **File**, and then click **Full Text Search**. Then click **Delete Index** from the Notes menu bar at the top of the screen.

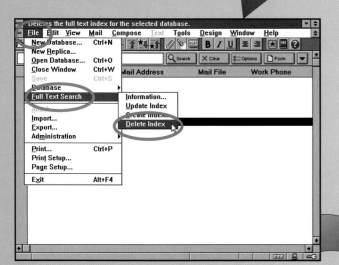

3 In the dialog box that appears, click the **Yes** button to verify the deletion of the full text index.

WHY WORRY?

You can always re-create a full text index on any database, should you need it again, by following the steps in Task 1 of this part.

TASK 24
Adding and Removing the Search Bar

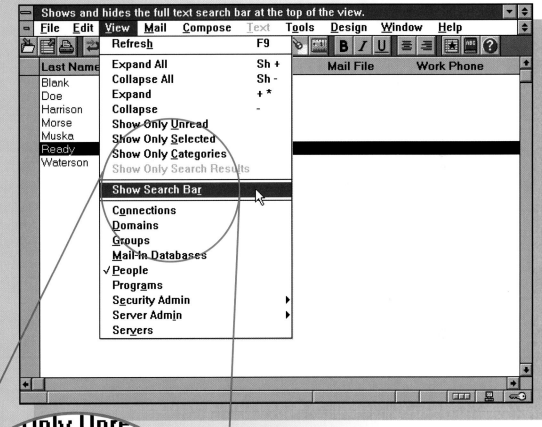

"Why would I do this?"

When a database has a full text index, you can run advanced text searches on it. Before you can run the searches, however, you must have access to the search bar. The search bar contains basic and advanced search options as well as an area to enter text. When you are not using it, you can hide the search bar from your database view. Notes automatically adds the search bar to databases that have full text indexes. This task shows you how to add and remove the search bar from a view in a database that has been previously indexed.

79

Task 24: Adding and Removing the Search Bar

1 Open the database to which you want to add the search bar by clicking the database icon on your workspace.

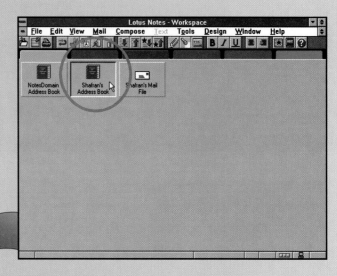

2 To add the search bar to your database, click **View** on the menu bar, and then click **Show Search Bar** to display the search bar.

3 Lotus Notes displays the search bar under the SmartIcon toolbar.

Click **View** on the menu bar, and then click **Show Search Bar** to remove the search bar from the view.

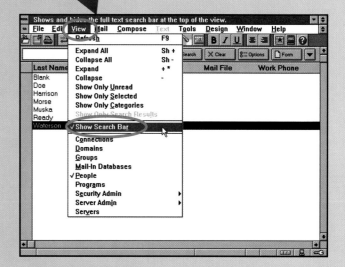

Running Text Searches with the Search Button

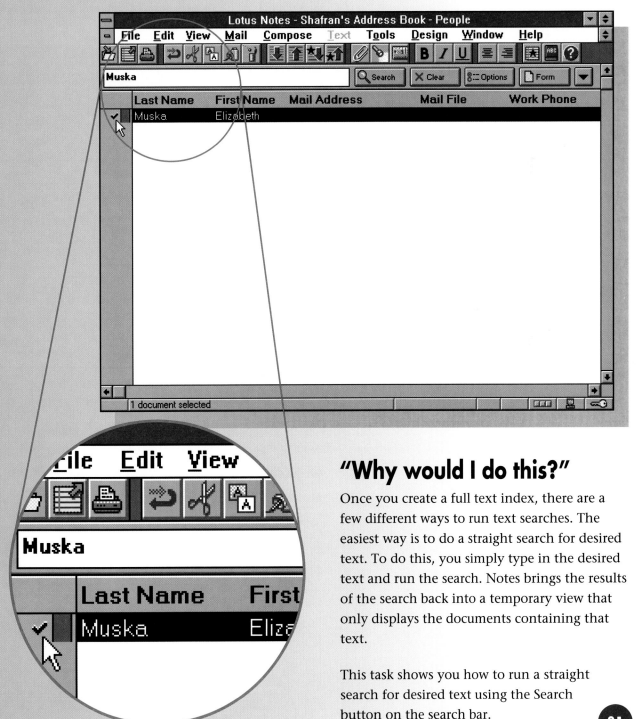

"Why would I do this?"

Once you create a full text index, there are a few different ways to run text searches. The easiest way is to do a straight search for desired text. To do this, you simply type in the desired text and run the search. Notes brings the results of the search back into a temporary view that only displays the documents containing that text.

This task shows you how to run a straight search for desired text using the Search button on the search bar.

Task 25: Running Text Searches with the Search Button

1 Open the database in which you want to run a straight text search by double-clicking the database icon from your Notes workspace. Ensure that your database has a full text index created, and the search bar is activated.

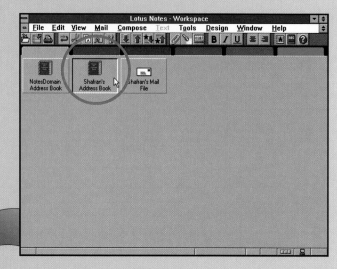

2 Enter the text you want to search for in the search bar's text box.

NOTE ▼

You can choose the Edit Find command from the menu bar to create more advanced text queries.

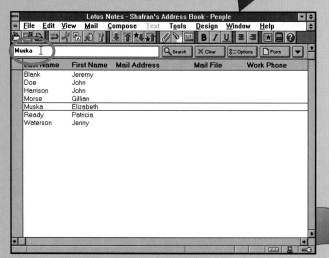

3 Click the **Search** button.

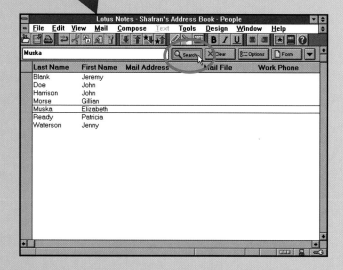

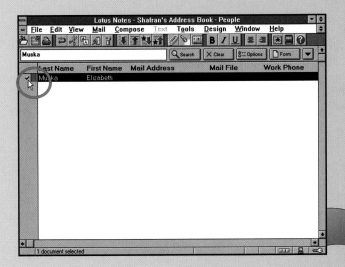

4 Scroll through the view that is created with the results of the search. You can select, copy, and delete documents in this search view.

5 Click the **Clear** button to erase this view and return to the previous one.

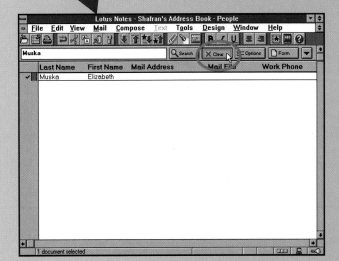

Running Text Searches with the Form Button

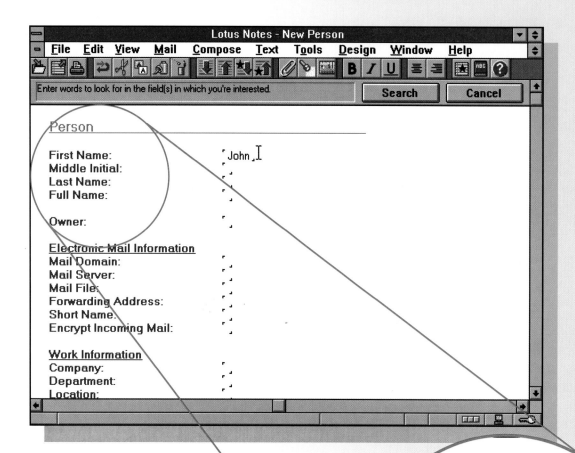

"Why would I do this?"

In addition to running a simple search of an entire database for desired text, you can search for information by using a form. Using a form lets you look for information in certain fields in a document.

This task shows you how to search for specific field information by using a form search on a database with a full text index.

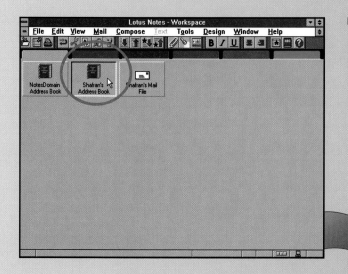

1 Open the database for which you want to run a full text search using the Form button by double-clicking the database icon on your workspace.

2 Click the **Form** button and select the document form you want to use for the search.

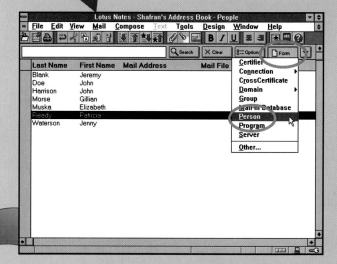

3 Enter the information you want to search for in the field(s) you want to look for it in. Notes builds a formula that searches for documents with that text in that particular field.

Task 26: Running Text Searches with the Form Button

4 Click the **Search** button to start the full text index search. Notes returns a view that contains the documents with the desired search text in the desired fields.

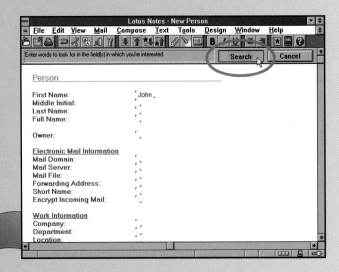

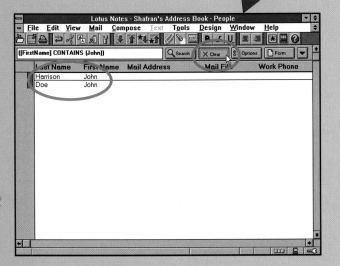

5 Click the **Clear** button to erase the results of the search and return to the previous view.

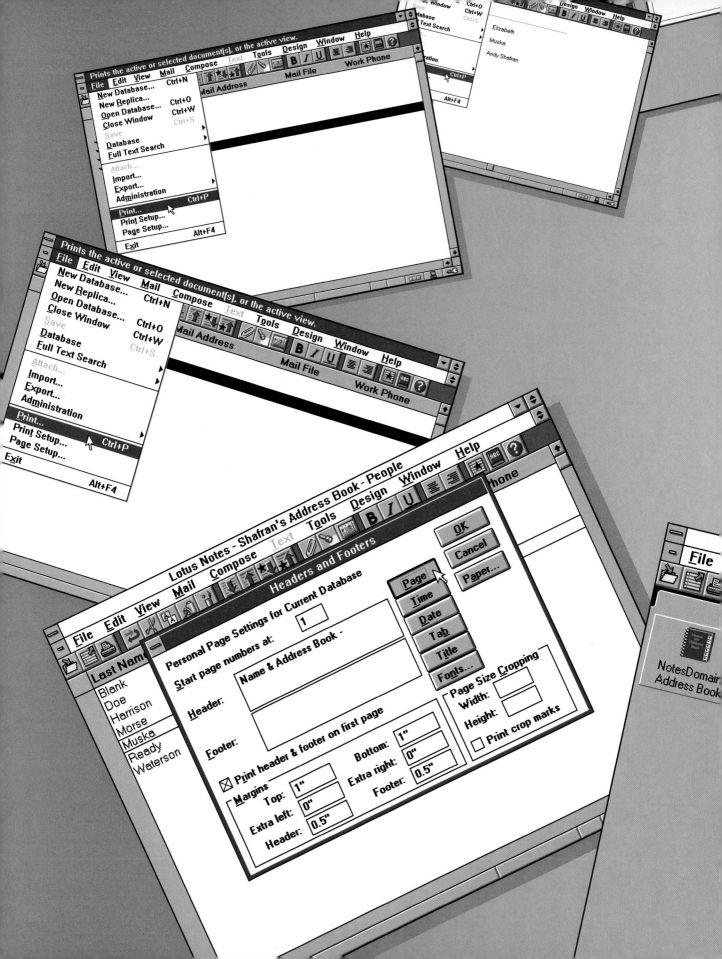

PART V

Using and Printing Documents

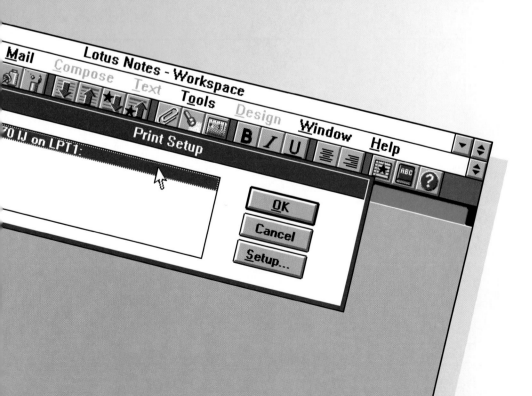

Part V: Using and Printing Documents

Even though Notes handles form routing, document authorization, and information sharing, you will often need to make printouts of information and views in various databases. Notes can print out any document within any database on any printer that is set up to run under Windows. You can print documents while reading them and print views. You can also add headers and footers to your printouts to help sort and label your pages. When designing databases, you can select sections of documents that Notes should not print and even have information printed out using a completely independent form.

The first step is to have a working printer under Windows. Because Notes' print functions are handled by Windows, you must have installed a printer under Windows for it to appear as an option under Notes. Once your printer is installed, you can use Notes to select it. Using a setup command, you can direct Notes to use any printer accessible by your machine.

After you have selected a printer for Notes to use, you can then print out your documents. Printing a document while reading it is easy. After entering the database and selecting the document to read, you can run a print function and Notes will send your output to the assigned printer.

If you need more than one document printed out at one time, or if you do not need to read the document you want to print, you can also make printouts from a view. After entering the database, you can use the mouse or space bar to select and deselect the documents you want to print.

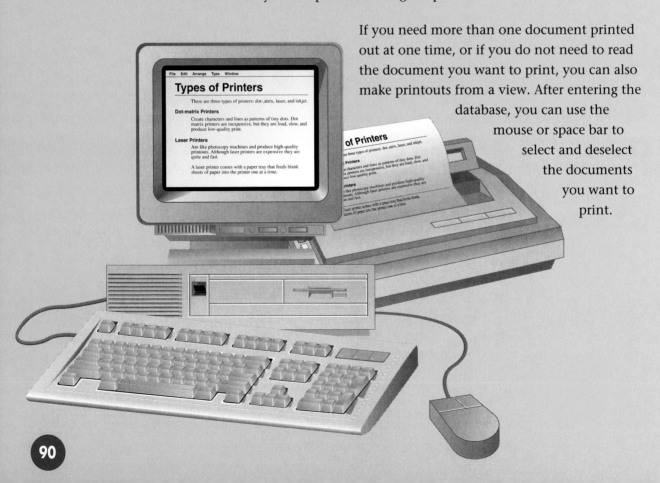

Once your selections are complete, you run a print function to send your documents to the printer.

Often, you will need to print out what you see at the view level rather than actual documents. When printing from a database, you simply choose the view option box and your view gets sent to your printer.

Notes can also add *headers* and *footers* to documents. Headers and footers are lines of text that appear on the top or bottom of all documents printed from a certain database. They can contain any text and can be any font, size, and color within your printer's capabilities.

Notes also lets you add special database information to headers and footers, such as page number, database name, time, and date.

The tasks in this part teach you how to select the printer you want to use, print a document while reading it, select and print multiple documents, print a view, and customize headers.

TASK 27
Selecting a Printer

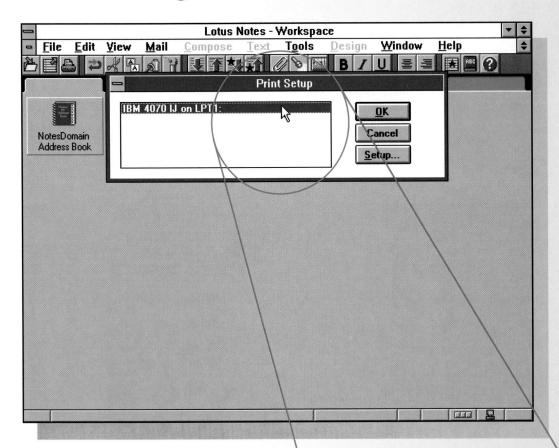

"Why would I do this?"

Because Notes runs under Windows, it has the same printing capabilities as other Windows applications, which means you can print output on any preinstalled, Windows-approved printer through Lotus Notes.

This task shows you how to configure Notes to use the correct preinstalled Windows printer for output.

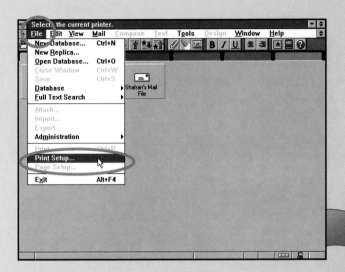

1 From anywhere within Notes, click **File** on the menu bar, and then click **Print Setup** to display a list of installed printers.

2 Scroll through the list of printers and select the printer you want to use for output by clicking it.

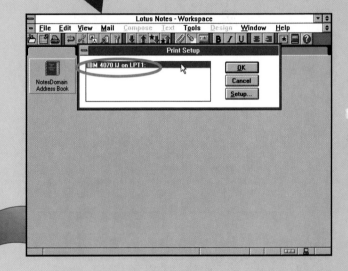

3 Click the **OK** button to select that printer for Notes output.

Printing a Document while Reading It

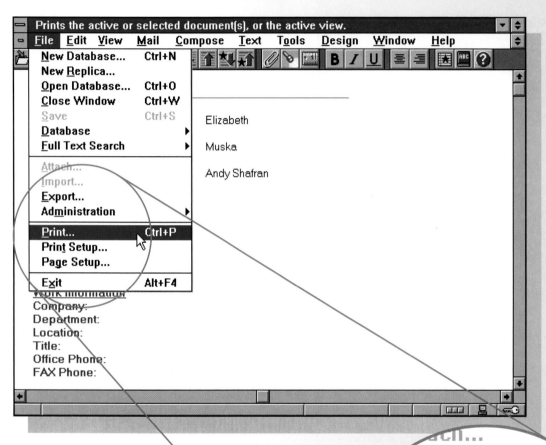

"Why would I do this?"

Occasionally, you will need hard copies of documents in various databases. Notes' printing functions include a built-in ability to print various documents while you are reading them.

This task shows you how to print a document in a Notes database while you are reading it.

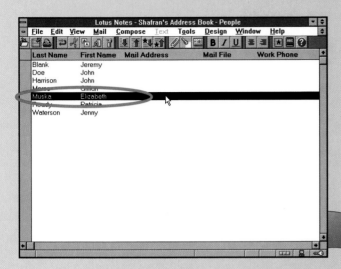

1 From a database, enter the document that you want to print by double-clicking it from the view level.

2 Click **File** on the menu bar and then click **Print** to display the File Print dialog box. You can specify the range of pages and number of copies you want to print from this dialog box.

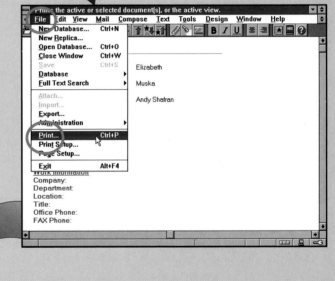

NOTE ▼

Ensure that you have selected the correct printer to output this document on. (See the preceding task for more details.)

3 Click the **OK** button to print the document on the previously selected printer.

Printing Documents from a View

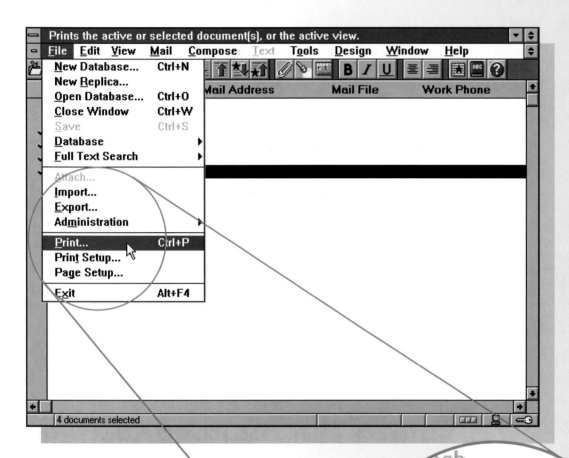

"Why would I do this?"

Another way of printing documents in Notes is to print from a view. If you print from a view, you can select and print multiple documents at one time. You also can select documents from multiple views within a database and print them all at once.

This task shows you how to select multiple documents from a Notes database and print them on the previously selected printer.

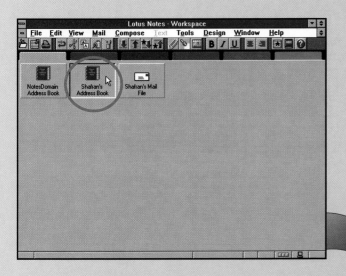

1 Enter the database from which you want to select and print multiple documents by double-clicking the database icon from your Notes workspace.

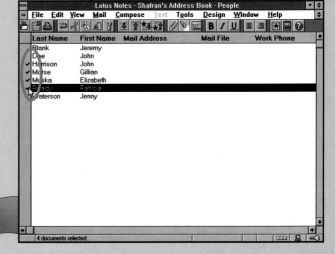

2 Select the documents you want to print by clicking once in the gray space to the left of the document. A check mark should appear next to each document you select.

> **NOTE** ▼
>
> You also can use the arrow keys to manipulate the cursor in the view, and use the space bar to select the document.

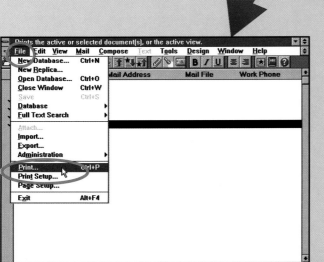

3 Click **File** on the menu bar, and then click **Print** to display the File Print dialog box.

> **NOTE** ▼
>
> Ensure that you have selected the correct printer to output this document on (see the first task in this part for more details).

Task 29: Printing Documents from a View

4 Select the way in which you would like Notes to separate your documents while printing. You can choose No Separation, an Extra Line, or Page Break by clicking the down arrow in the Document Separation box.

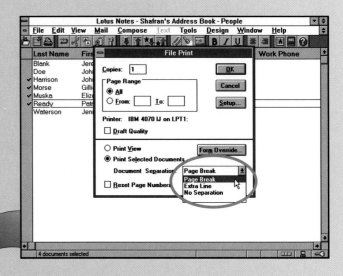

5 Click the **OK** button to print the documents on the currently selected printer.

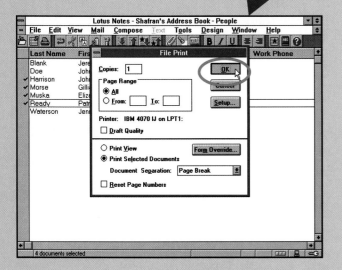

Printing a View

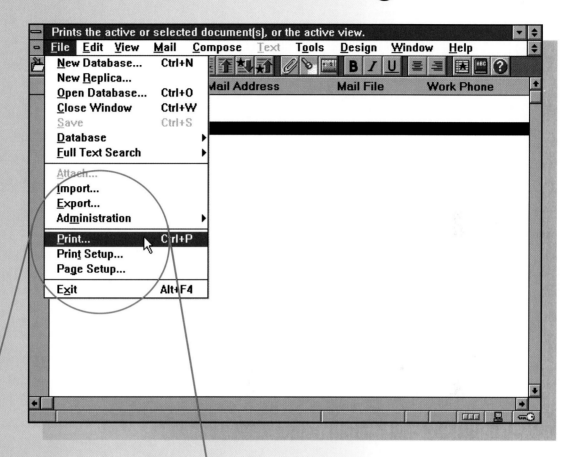

"Why would I do this?"

Sometimes you might want to print out a view rather than separate documents. You may need to have a summary of database information for a presentation or for billing and tracking purposes. In Notes, you can print out any customized views you want.

This task shows you how to print a view from a Notes database on the previously selected printer.

Task 30: Printing a View

1 Open the database from which you want to print the view by double-clicking its icon from the Notes workspace.

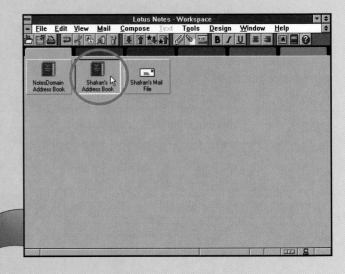

2 Click the **View** command on the menu bar, and then select the view you want to print by clicking it.

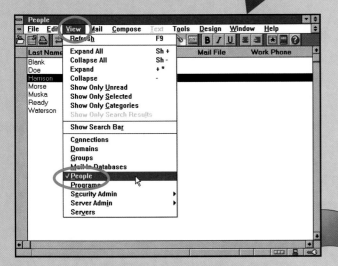

3 Click **File** on the menu bar and then click **Print** to display the File Print dialog box.

NOTE ▼

Ensure that you have selected the correct printer to output this document on.

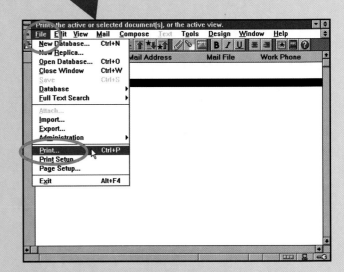

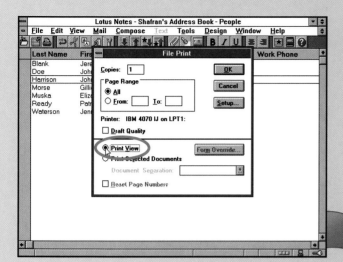

4 Click the **Print View** radio button to select it.

5 Click the **OK** button to print the view on your previously selected printer.

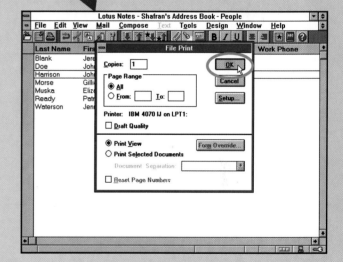

TASK 31

Creating Page Headers and Footers

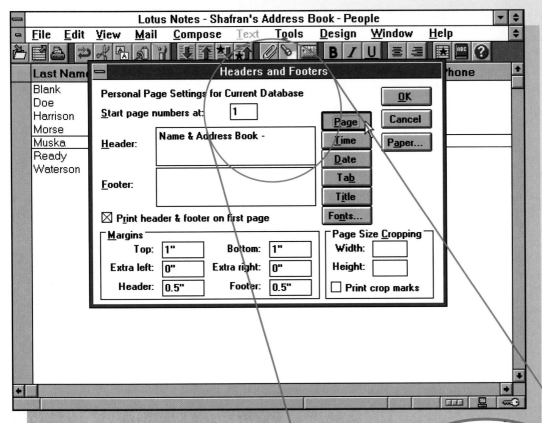

"Why would I do this?"

Sometimes when you print out documents and/or views, you need to have titles on your output. Using Notes, you can add page headers and page footers to all pages of your printout. The header and footer can be any font, size, or color, and can include page numbers, the date, and the time. This task shows you how to add a simple header and footer to documents that are printed from a certain database.

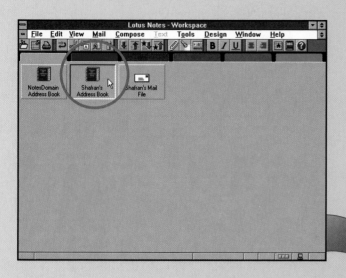

1 Enter or select the database where you want to create a header or footer by using your left mouse button.

2 Click **File** on the menu bar, and then click **Page Setup** to display the Headers and Footers dialog box.

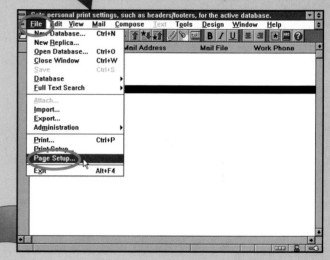

3 In the Header text box, enter the text you want in the header. For example, type **Name & Address Book** - .

Task 31: Creating Page Headers and Footers

4 Click the **Page** button to add the page number to the header.

> **NOTE** ▼
>
> You can press the other buttons to include time, date, tabs, and database title, as well as change the size and font of the header.

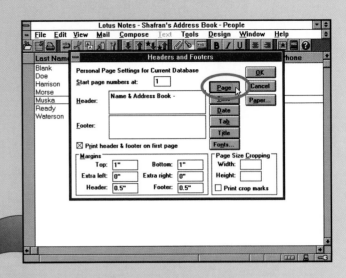

5 After clicking in the Footer text box, add the time variable to your footer by clicking the **Time** button.

6 Click the **OK** button to accept the changes you made to the header and footer.

> **NOTE** ▼
>
> Any changes you make in the header or footer only take effect in the particular database you are in, and only when you print from your local workstation.

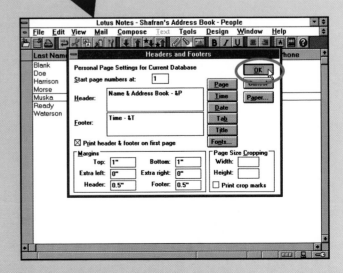

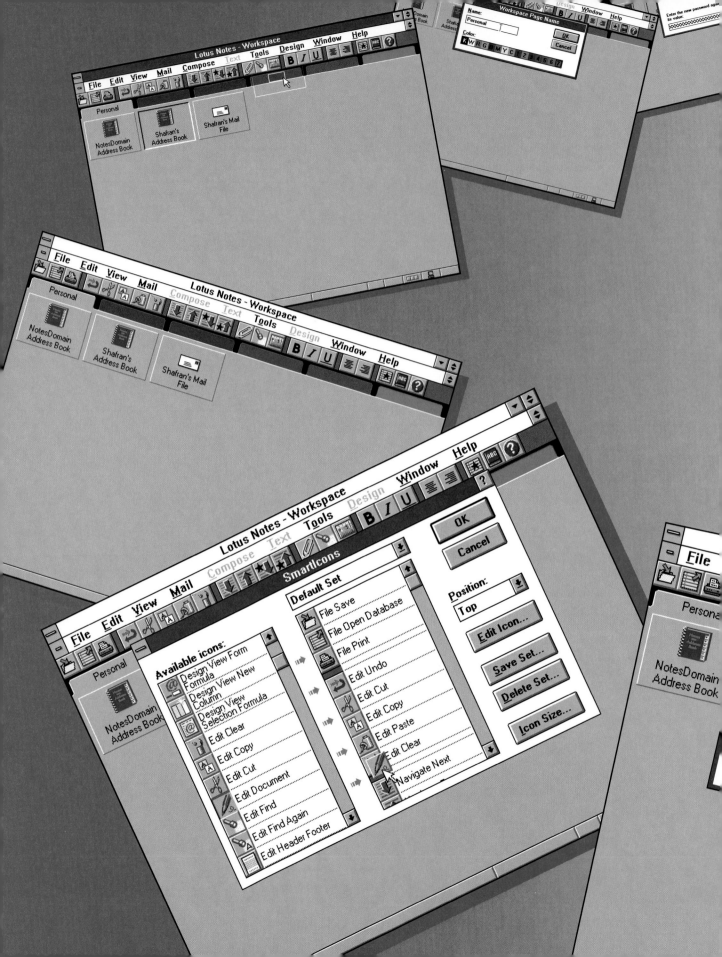

PART VI

Securing and Customizing the Notes Workspace

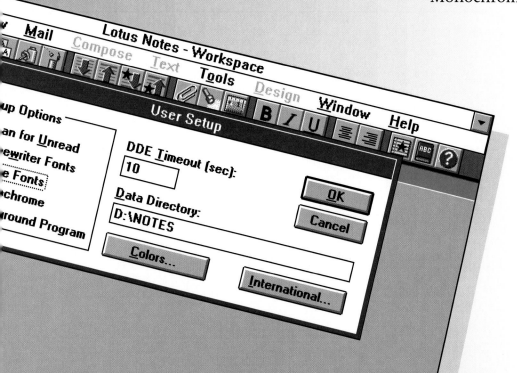

This task teaches you how to customize your Notes workspace. Before you customize your workspace, however, you should change your password. Most system administrators set user passwords to some default value, and encourage users to change their passwords as soon as they can. Notes makes it easy for you to change your personal password whenever you like.

One easy way to customize your workspace is to place text labels on all six file folder tabs to help with organization. You can also easily move databases back and forth from one file folder page to another. Keeping similar databases grouped together makes data easier to find.

Using SmartIcons can make Notes easier to use. SmartIcons offer an easy, one-click method for running most Notes functions. You can use any of the seven default sets of SmartIcons; it's easy to switch between default sets of SmartIcons at any point in Notes.

If none of the default sets of SmartIcons meets your needs, you can create a customized set. You can base your new set on one of the default sets, or create a new one from scratch. Once you create the new set, you can access it just as easily as Notes' default sets.

If you have a very high-resolution monitor, you may find it difficult to read Notes text sometimes. You can customize Notes to alleviate this problem by enlarging the default font size slightly to make it easier to read the screen on certain high-resolution monitors.

If you use a laptop or monochrome screen, some Notes Windows may be hard to read because of the way colors appear on your monitor. You can inform Notes that you are running on a monochrome screen, and the program will convert all databases and colors into an easy-to-read gray scale for you. This gray scale makes all databases easy-to-read, regardless of the colors in them.

This part shows you how to change your personal Notes password, label and organize your desktop and folders, change and create SmartIcons sets, and customize Notes for monochrome and high-resolution monitors.

TASK 32

Changing Your Lotus Notes Personal Password

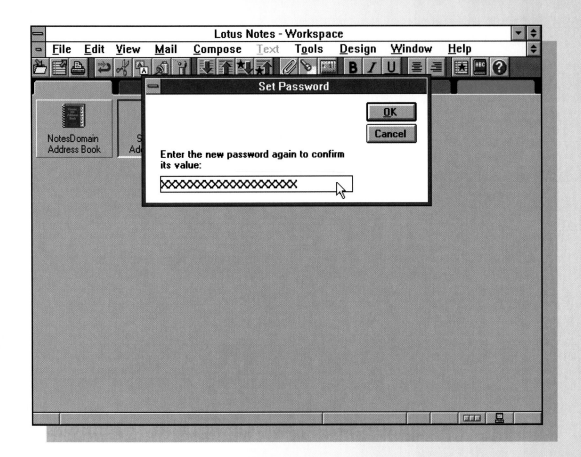

"Why would I do this?"

Although you don't need a Notes password to access information located on your machine, you do need one to access information on your Notes network. Your system administrator gives you your first password, but you can change it to be any set of characters you want. This task shows you how to change your Notes password.

Task 32: Changing Your Lotus Notes Personal Password

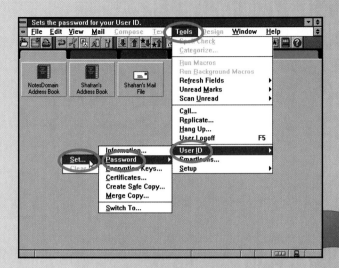

1 From anywhere in Notes, click **Tools** on the menu bar, and then click **User ID**. Then click **Password**, and then click **Set**.

2 Lotus Notes displays the Enter Password dialog box. Type your *current* Notes password in the text box, and then click **OK**.

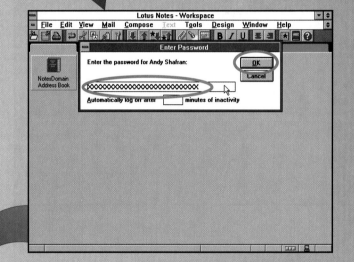

> **NOTE** ▼
>
> A random number of X's appear in the prompt for each character you type in. These letters have nothing to do with your password; they are just another level of Notes security.

3 Notes displays a Set Password dialog box. Type your *new* password in the text box.

Task 32: Changing Your Lotus Notes Personal Password

4 Click **OK** after you enter your new password.

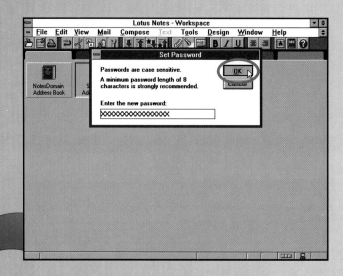

5 Enter your new password again to verify its spelling.

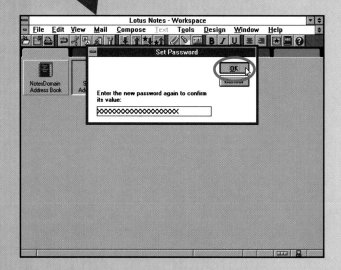

6 Click **OK** when you have entered your new password again to complete the password change.

Labeling the Folders

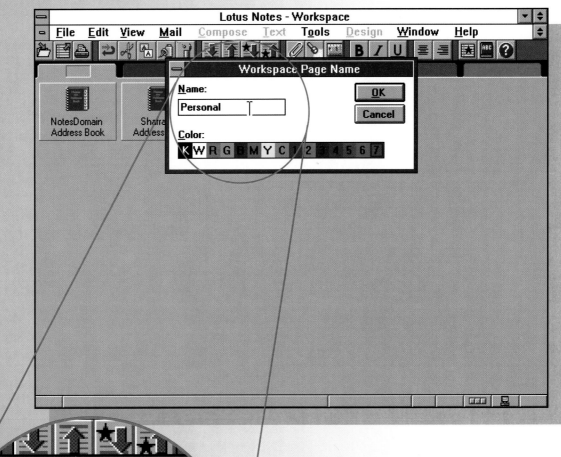

"Why would I do this?"

After using Notes for awhile, you may start to accumulate many databases on your workspace. In order to keep track of all these databases, you may want to organize your file folders by various subjects. Labeling your file folders will make it easier to locate various databases. This task shows you how to label a file folder.

Task 33: Labeling the Folders

1 From your Notes workspace, double-click the file folder tab to which you want to add a label. The Workspace Page Name dialog box appears on-screen.

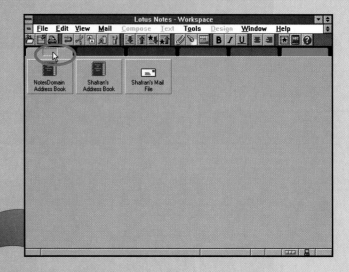

2 Enter a name for the file folder in the Name text box. Click **OK** with your mouse to save the new file folder label.

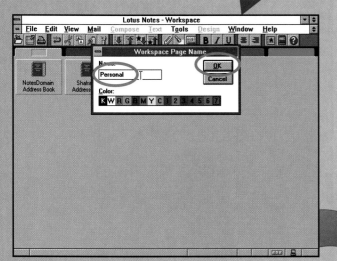

3 Notice the new file folder label. The color will be gray because the current file folder label is always gray no matter which page you are on.

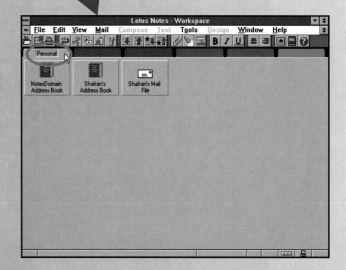

TASK 34

Moving Databases between Folders

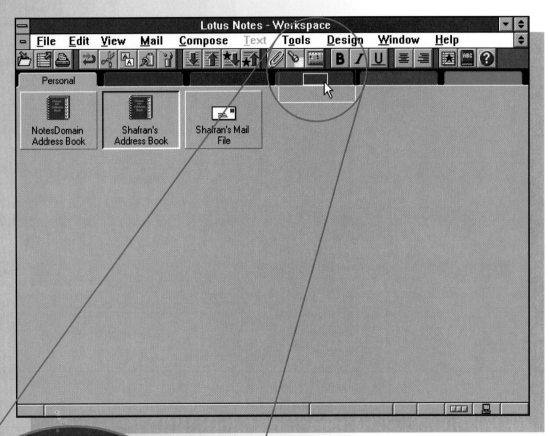

"Why would I do this?"

Notes automatically adds new databases to your current database page. Sometimes you may want to move those databases to different file folder pages to help you keep organized. By organizing the databases, you can customize your Notes workspace to fit your needs. This task shows you how to select and move Notes databases from one file folder page to another.

Task 34: Moving Databases between Folders

1 From your Notes workspace, select the database you want to move by clicking its icon.

NOTE ▼

You can select multiple databases by pressing the Shift key while selecting the database icons.

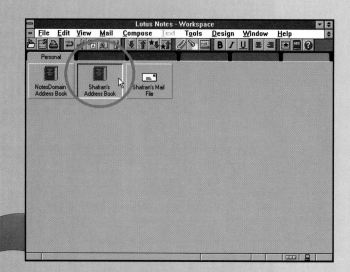

2 While pressing the mouse button, drag the database icon to the tab of the file folder page you want to move it to by moving the mouse. An outline box should appear on the tab.

3 Release the mouse button to complete the database move.

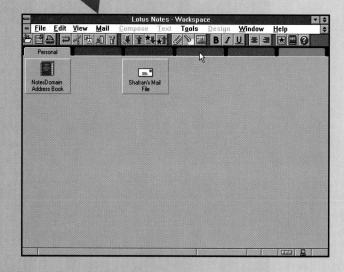

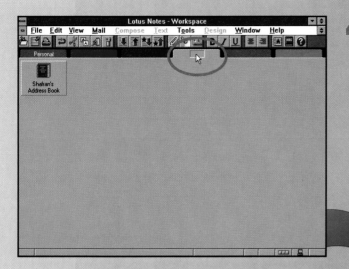

4 Click the tab of the file folder to which you moved the database to observe the database page with your newly moved database on it.

5 Select and drag the databases around the page to arrange your workspace the way you want.

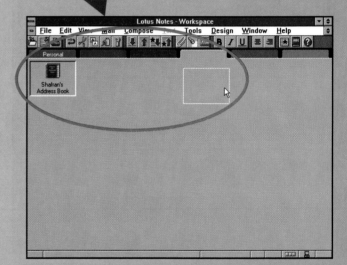

Changing to a Different Default Set of SmartIcons

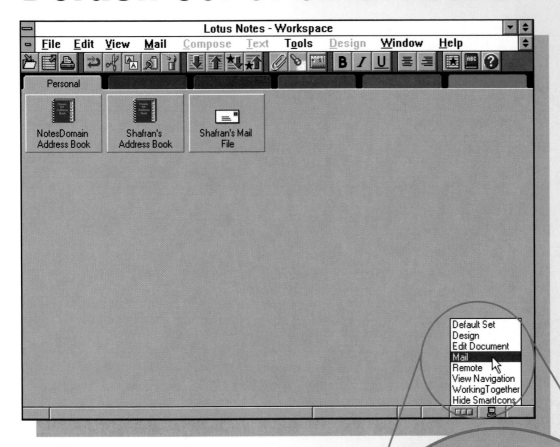

"Why would I do this?"

SmartIcons are buttons you click to run Notes functions. The set of SmartIcons on your screen is probably a default set created when Notes was installed. There are seven default sets of SmartIcons grouped together for various parts of Notes.

This task shows you how to easily change your set of SmartIcons to another default set that comes with Notes.

Task 35: Changing to a Different Default Set of SmartIcons

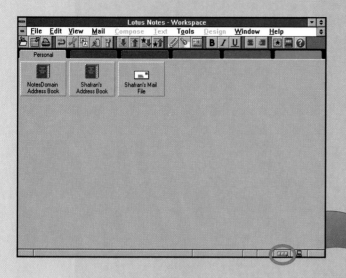

1 From your Notes workspace, click the small icon in the bottom right corner of the page that resembles three blue blocks in a row.

2 From the list that appears on-screen, click any set of SmartIcons except `Default Set` to see new SmartIcons appear at the top of your screen. For example, click **Mail**.

WHY WORRY?

If you want your default set of SmartIcons back, repeat this process and click Default Set for them to reappear.

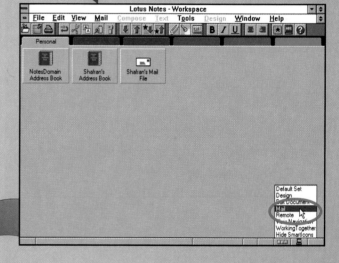

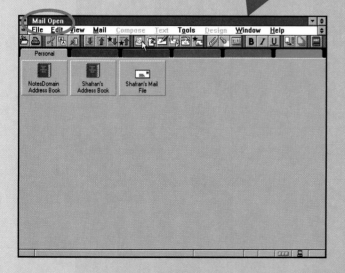

3 Examine the new set of SmartIcons by holding down the *right* mouse button on a SmartIcon to get a description of it in the Notes title bar.

TASK 36
Creating a Custom Set of SmartIcons

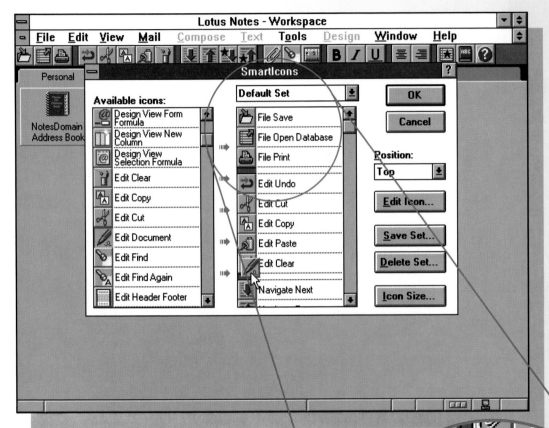

"Why would I do this?"

Notes comes with seven sets of SmartIcons.
They are all customized for various functions
such as reading mail, and working on a laptop.
You may enjoy using SmartIcons, but find that
none of the default sets contains all of the
SmartIcons you use on a regular basis. You can
easily create your own set of SmartIcons to
place at the top of the Notes screen. This task
explains how to add the SmartIcons you want
to an existing set of SmartIcons.

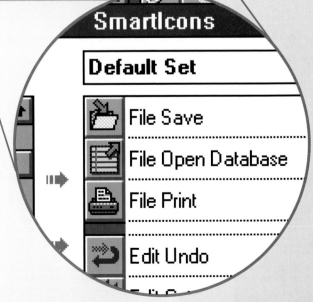

Task 36: Creating a Custom Set of SmartIcons

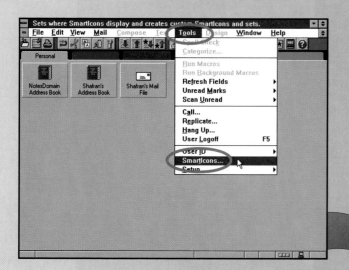

1 Click **Tools** on the Notes menu bar, and then click **SmartIcons** to display the SmartIcons dialog box.

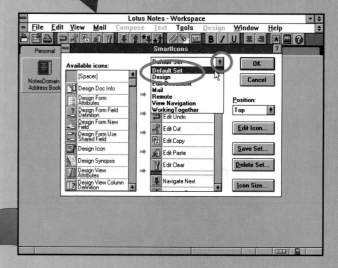

2 Change your current set of SmartIcons to the default set by clicking the down arrow from the box below the SmartIcon title bar and selecting **Default Set** from the list.

3 Scroll through the Available icons list until you find an icon you want to add to your default set of SmartIcons.

Task 36: Creating a Custom Set of SmartIcons

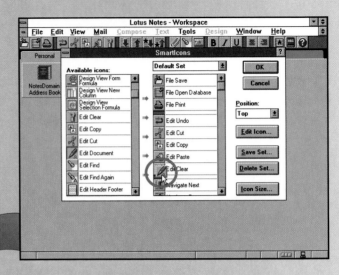

4 Move the mouse pointer to the icon you want to add. For example, add the Edit Document icon. Hold down the *left* mouse button and drag the icon to the default set of icons by moving the mouse.

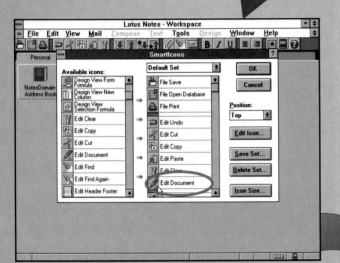

5 Release the mouse button when you have placed the cursor with the icon in the spot you want to place the new SmartIcon. You can use the spacer SmartIcon to insert blank spaces in your SmartIcon bar. If you have too many SmartIcons per set, they will not all be displayed on-screen.

NOTE ▼

You can remove SmartIcons by dragging them from the set that you are currently editing.

6 After you add all the new SmartIcons you want and remove the ones that are no longer necessary, click the **Save Set** button to display the Save Set of SmartIcons dialog box.

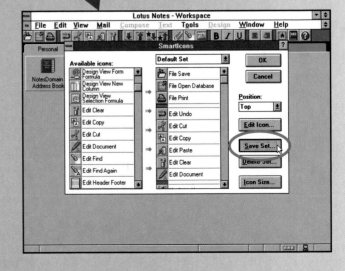

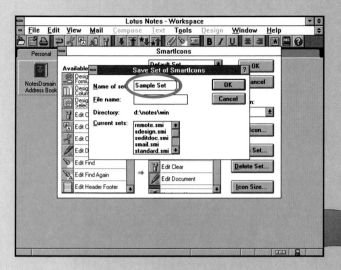

7 Enter a new name for the set of icons in the Name of set text box so you can tell the difference between the sets of icons when you want to change sets.

8 Enter a new file name for the set of icons in the File name text box so that your new set of icons does not overwrite the default set that came with Notes.

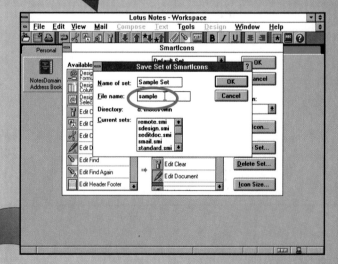

9 Click the **OK** button to save the new set of SmartIcons.

Task 36: Creating a Custom Set of SmartIcons

10 Select an option from the Position drop-down list box to specify where you want the SmartIcons to appear on-screen.

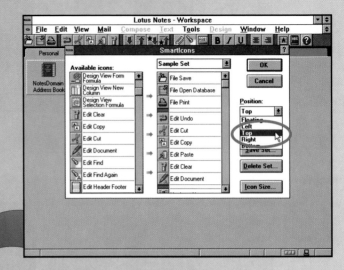

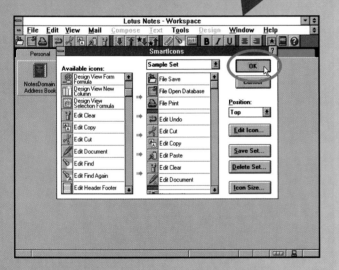

11 Click the **OK** button to close the SmartIcons dialog box.

Changing to Larger Default Font Sizes

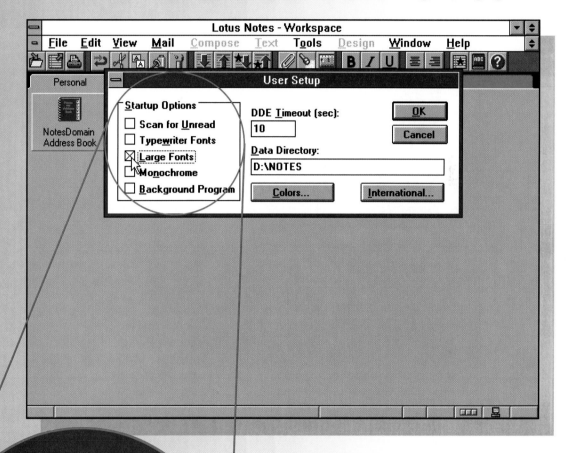

"Why would I do this?"

Notes can run on all types of Windows-compatible machines with VGA resolution. Occasionally, when you run Notes at a higher than VGA resolution, Notes text can appear small and difficult to read. Although you can enlarge many databases' text sizes, it may be easier to customize your Notes workspace for your databases. This task shows you how to set up Notes so it runs with slightly larger font sizes, making it easier to read screen text on high-resolution monitors.

Task 37: Changing to Larger Default Font Sizes

1 Click **Tools** on the Notes menu bar, and then click **Setup**. Then click **User**.

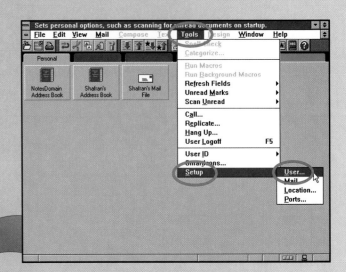

2 In the User Setup dialog box, select the **Large Fonts** check box by clicking it to change the default font size.

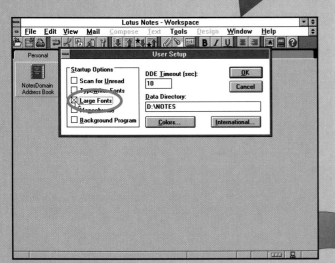

> **NOTE** ▼
>
> You can use the space bar to select the check box as well.

3 Click **OK** to save the changes to Notes.

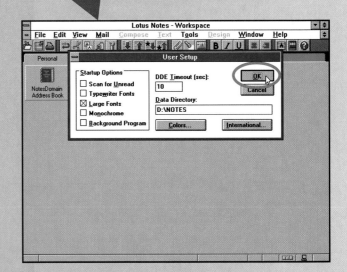

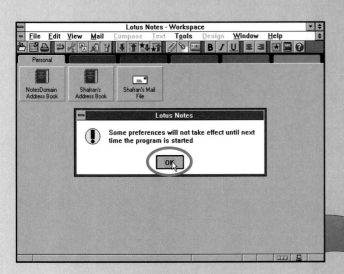

4 Click **OK** to close the dialog box that notifies you to exit the program for the changes to take effect.

5 Click **File** on the Notes menu bar, and then click **Exit** to exit Notes.

WHY WORRY?

Notes prompts you to save any unsaved windows if you try to exit before saving your work.

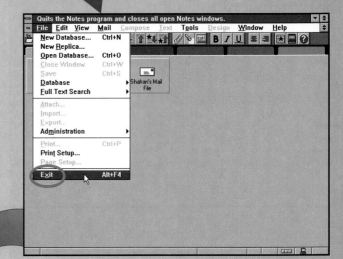

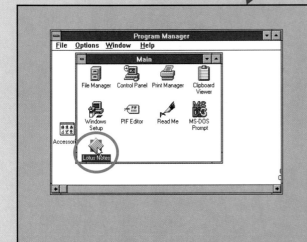

6 Double-click the Notes icon in Program Manager to restart Notes so that the changes you made can take effect.

Customizing Notes for Use on a Monochrome Screen

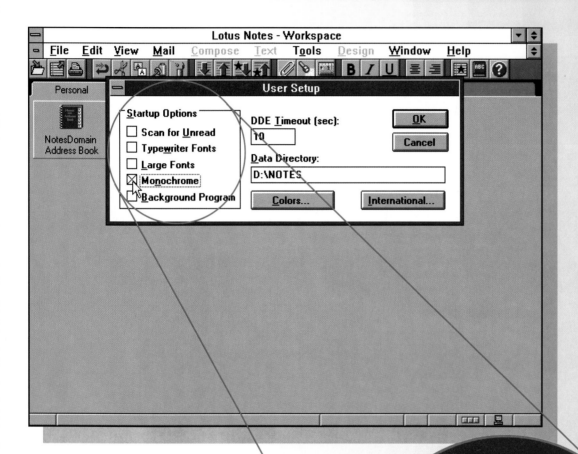

"Why would I do this?"

Notes can run on laptop machines that have modems installed; it can also run on machines that use monochrome VGA screens. Sometimes certain databases can be hard to read on monitors that do not display colors, if your Notes workspace does not know to display only in monochrome mode. This task customizes Notes to run on a machine that does not display color screens. It tells Notes to show screens in shades of gray.

Startup Options

☐ Scan for **U**nread
☐ Type**w**riter Fonts
☐ **L**arge Fonts
☒ Mon**o**chrome
☐ **B**ackground Progra

Task 38: Customizing Notes for Use on a Monochrome Screen

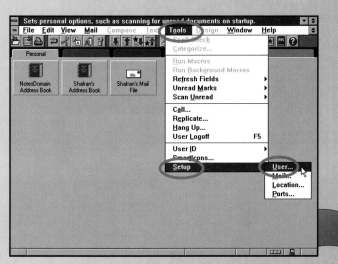

Click **Tools** on the Notes menu bar, and then click **Setup**. Then click **User**.

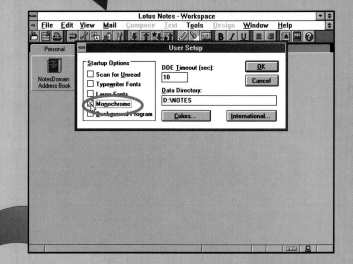

In the User Setup dialog box, select the **Monochrome** check box by clicking it to change the default font color scheme.

> **NOTE** ▼
>
> You can use the space bar to select the check box as well.

Click the **OK** button to save the changes to Notes.

4 Click the **OK** button to close the dialog box that notifies you that you must exit the program for the changes to take effect.

5 Click **File** from the Notes menu bar, and then click **Exit** to exit Notes.

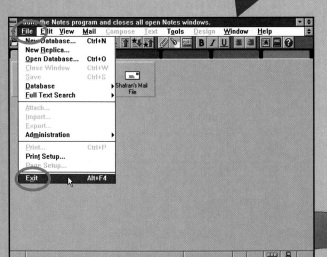

WHY WORRY?

Notes prompts you to save any unsaved windows if you try to exit Notes before saving your work.

6 Double-click the Notes icon in Program Manager to restart Notes so that the changes you made can take effect.

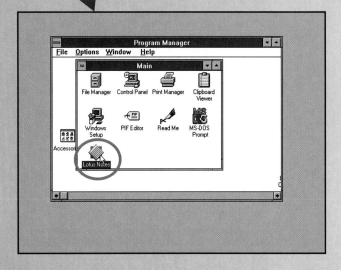

PART VII

Developing Notes Databases

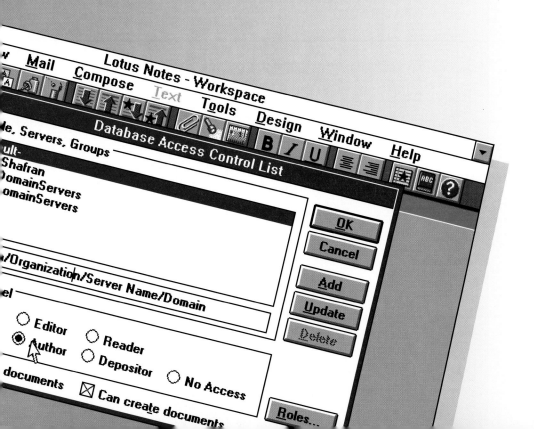

Part VII: Developing Notes Databases

All Notes applications consist of one or more databases with specific functions. These databases are built one at a time by Notes developers and designers.

The first step to designing a Notes database is to decide what the purpose of the database is. You need to decide whether you are building an application with several databases, or a self-contained project. This decision helps you choose which default template you want to use (if any), and helps you plan your database functions.

Building new databases is a great way to become even more comfortable with the Notes interface and various features. Creating a new database lets you see Notes from a design perspective.

When you create a database, you can either create a database from scratch or use a database template. When you create a new database from scratch, you go through the entire database creation process and learn the fundamentals of forms and views. The templates already have view and forms in them that can be customized to fit various needs. Notes comes with 17 templates, which you can use to create many different types of databases.

After creating a database, you should add a creative icon to it. You can use bit-mapped images pasted from the Windows Clipboard or design your own with the built-in Notes icon editor.

The next step in creating a database is creating forms. A *form* is what you use to compose documents to populate the database. When you create the form, Notes gives you a completely blank screen for you to customize. You edit the form by adding appropriate fields for the information to be stored in this form. You can add all types of fields to store different types of information. Fields can contain text, dates, graphics, names, tables, and charts.

Once your form is completed, you need to create a view so you can track your composed documents. When you create a view, you add columns that can display almost any fields in the form. After you save your view, you have a functional database. You can now add more forms and views to your database to customize it to your liking.

Notes has a macro language that allows you to take advantage of many Notes features and functions in your database forms and views. Using the macro language is usually more advanced design work, but you should be aware of it.

The last step in creating your database is checking the user security levels. You can add users one at a time to give certain access to certain users, or you can set a default security level for all users to have when accessing that database. Notes security is another complex issue that only starts with the database.

This part will show you how to create a new database from scratch. It shows you how to create an icon, form, field, and view for the database as well as update the security levels.

Creating a Database

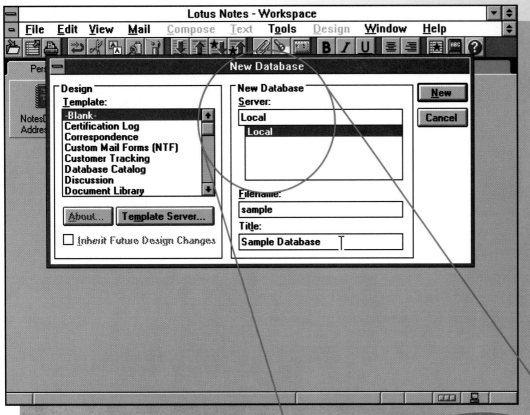

"Why would I do this?"

After learning how to access and use databases, you may want to learn how to build your own. Building your own database from scratch is a good way to become familiar with Notes database design functions.

This task shows you how to create a database from your Notes workspace.

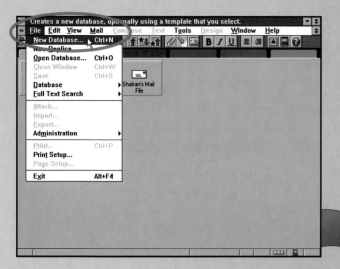

1 Click **File** on the Notes menu bar, and then click **New Database** to open the New Database dialog box.

2 Select the template you want to base your new database on from the Template list box. Each template comes with its own forms and views that are configured for a specific purpose. For this task, click **-Blank-** to create an empty database.

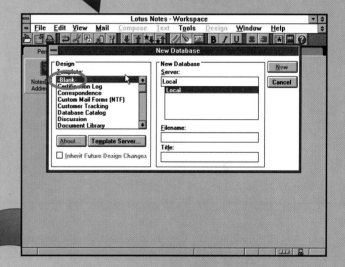

3 Enter the server on which you want to place your new database in the Server text box. For this task, make sure **Local** is in the text box.

Task 39: Creating a Database

4 Enter the file name for your database in the Filename text box. For this task, type **sample**. Notes automatically adds the file extension (.NSF) to your file name for you.

> **NOTE** ▼
>
> Your file name can only be eight characters long.

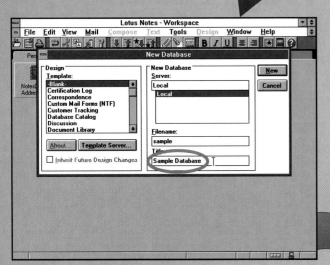

5 Enter the description of your database in the **Title** text box. This text appears as a label for your Notes database on your workspace. For this task, type **Sample Database**.

6 Click the **New** button to create the new database.

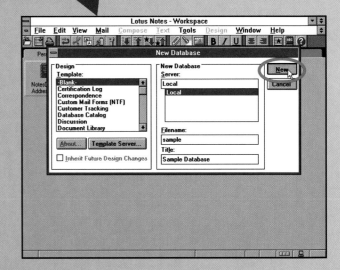

Creating an Icon for a Database

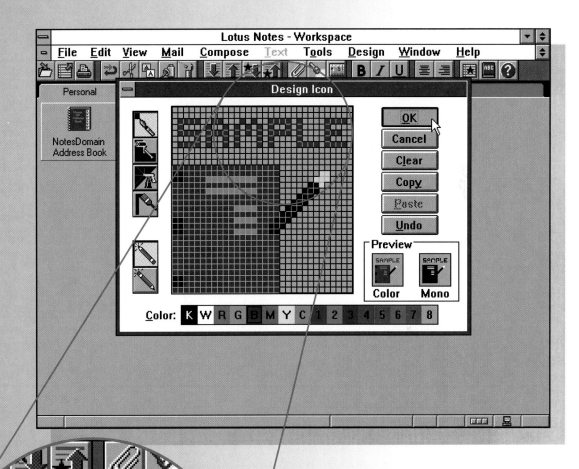

"Why would I do this?"

When you create a new database, no default icon is created with it. You can design an icon by using the icon editor built into Notes. You can create images and designs in many colors with this feature.

This task shows you how to use the icon editor to design your own Notes database icon.

139

Task 40: Creating an Icon for a Database

1 From your Notes workspace, select the database for which you want to create the icon by clicking it.

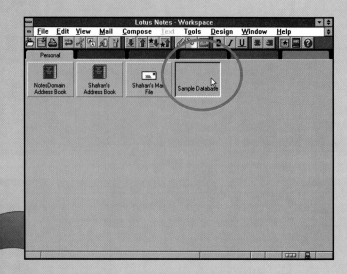

2 Click **Design** on the Notes menu bar, and then click **Icon** to open the Design Icon dialog box.

3 Use the straight line drawing tool to draw outlines for the images you want to create with the icon editor.

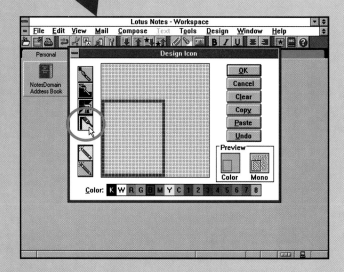

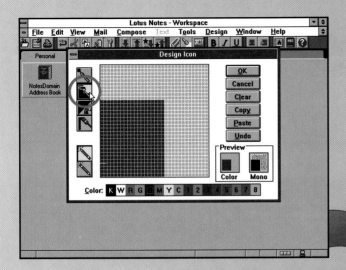

4 Use the fill drawing tool to fill in enclosed objects in your icon when using the icon editor.

5 Use the square by square drawing tool to add details to your icon when using the icon editor.

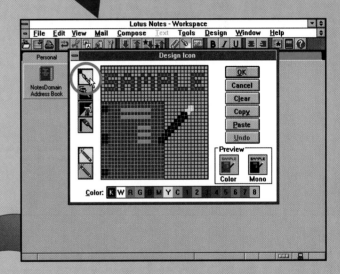

6 When you are finished designing your new database icon, click the **OK** button to save the image.

Creating a New Form

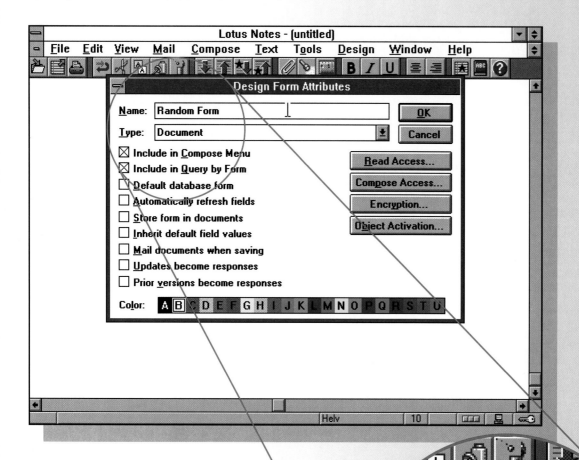

"Why would I do this?"

You must create a form so that you can enter information in your database. When you design a form, you are given a blank screen to customize in whichever way you want. You must enter a title for the form to be able to save and compose a document with that form.

This task shows you how to create a new form in a database.

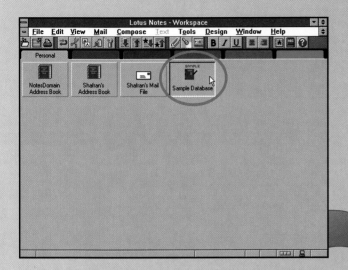

1 From your Notes workspace, open the database in which you want to create a new form by double-clicking the database icon.

2 Click **Design** on the Notes menu bar, and then click **Forms** to display the Design Forms dialog box.

3 Click the **New** button to create a new form in that database.

Task 41: Creating a New Form

4 Click **Design** from the Notes menu bar, and then click **Form Attributes** to display the Design Form Attributes dialog box.

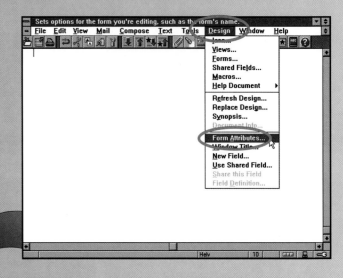

5 Enter a title for the form in the Name text box. For this task, type **Random Form**. Random Form will now appear on the Compose menu for this database.

6 Click the **OK** button to close the Design Form Attributes dialog box.

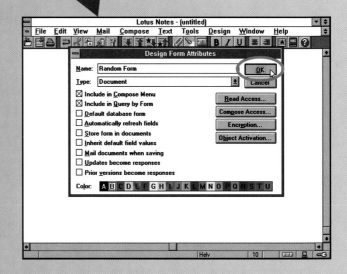

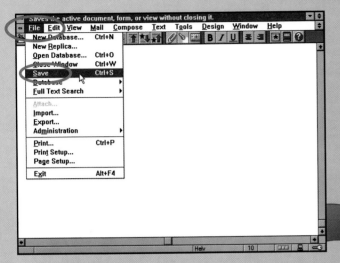

7 Click **File** from the Notes menu bar, and then click **Save** to save the new form.

8 To exit the form, double-click it with your *right* mouse button to return to the previous screen.

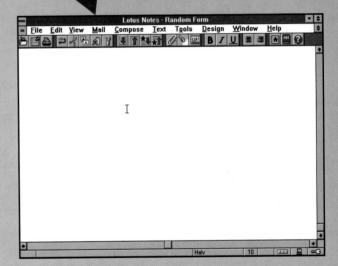

TASK 42

Adding a Field to a Form

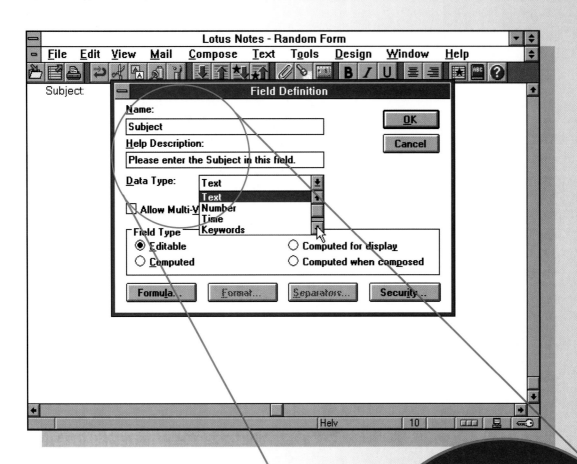

"Why would I do this?"

For a form to be useful, it must have fields so that people using the form can enter the correct information. This task shows you how to add a field to your form.

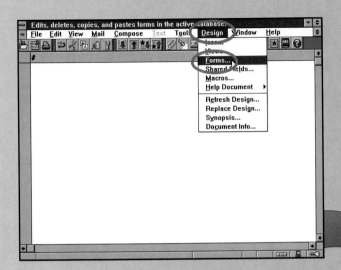

Click **Design** on the Notes menu bar, and then click **Forms** to display the Design Forms dialog box.

In the Forms list box, double-click the form you want to add fields to.

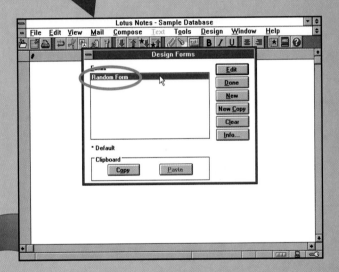

On your blank Notes form, type in labeling text. For this task, type **Subject:**.

Task 42: Adding a Field to a Form

4 Click **Design** on the Notes menu bar, and then click **New Field** to create a new field.

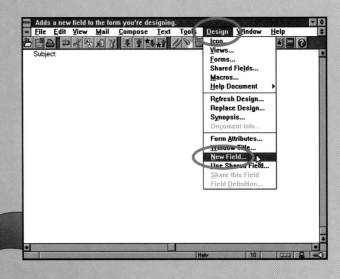

5 Click **OK** in the Design New Field dialog box to accept the default option and create a field to be used only in this form.

6 In the Field Definition dialog box that appears, enter a title for the field in the Name text box. For this task, type **Subject**.

> **NOTE** ▼
>
> Each field on a form must have a unique name. No spaces are permitted in field names.

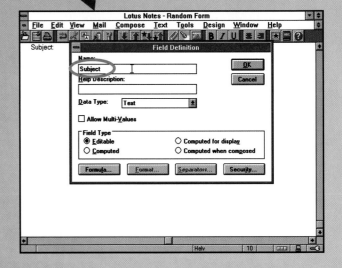

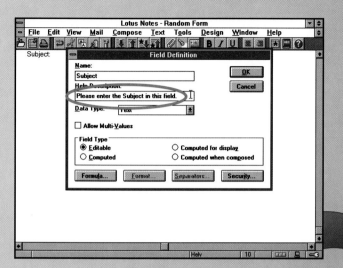

7 Enter text in the Help Description text box. This text appears at the bottom of the screen when a user composes a document using this form.

NOTE ▼

To ensure that you can see the help text for fields, click **View** and then click **Show field help** from the menu bar while reading a Notes document to toggle the field help text on and off.

8 From the Data Type drop-down list, select a field type. For this task, select **Text**. The following table explains all the field types.

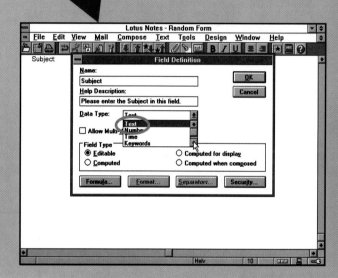

Field Type Name	Allowable Contents
Text	Any text you can create on a keyboard.
Number	Any numeric value (commas and decimals permitted).
Time	Any time and/or date value (must be separated by '/' marks).
Keywords	A list of specific entries that the user can select.
Rich Text	Any mix of characters, graphics, and charts.
Names	Valid Notes user names.
Author Names	The names of the users who are allowed to edit this document.
Reader Names	The names of Notes users who are allowed to read this document.
Section	A subset of the Notes documents that can be edited by specific users.

Task 42: Adding a Field to a Form

9 Click the **OK** button to create the new field. Follow the preceding steps to add a Number and Date field.

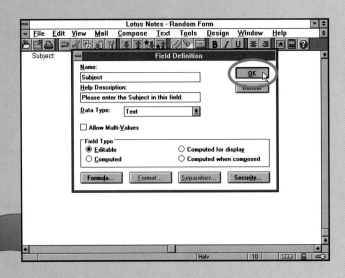

10 Click **File** on the Notes menu bar, and then click **Save** to save the form with the new field.

11 To exit the form, double-click it with your *right* mouse button.

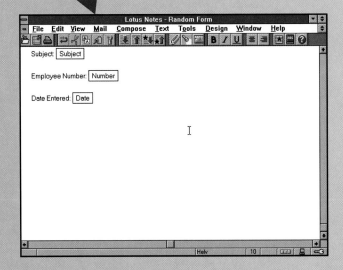

Creating a View

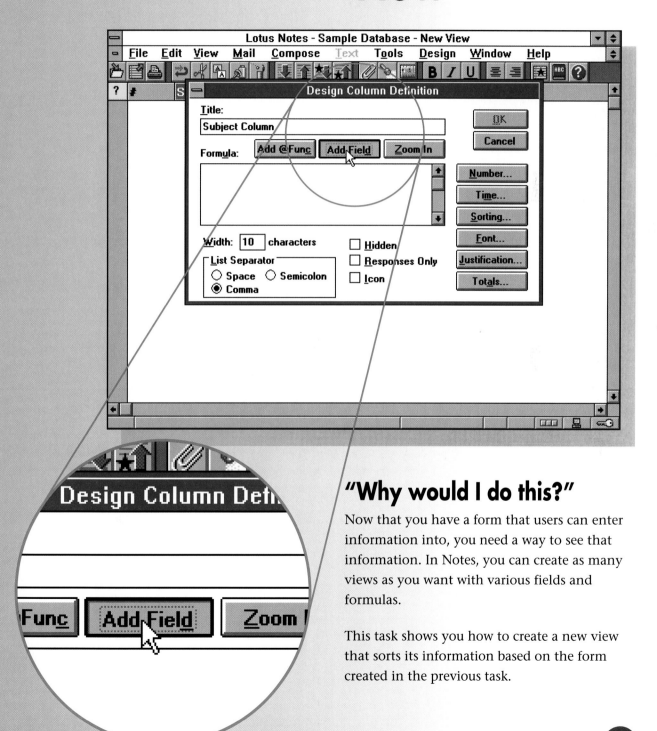

"Why would I do this?"

Now that you have a form that users can enter
information into, you need a way to see that
information. In Notes, you can create as many
views as you want with various fields and
formulas.

This task shows you how to create a new view
that sorts its information based on the form
created in the previous task.

Task 43: Creating a View

1 From your Notes workspace, open the database you want to create a new view in by double-clicking its icon.

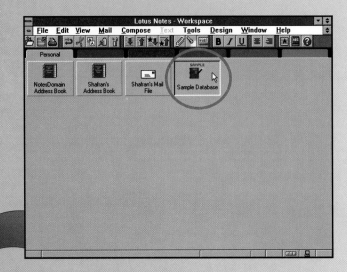

2 Click **Design** from the Notes menu bar, and then click **Views** to display the Design Views dialog box.

3 In the Views list box, double-click the ***(untitled)** view to edit that default database view.

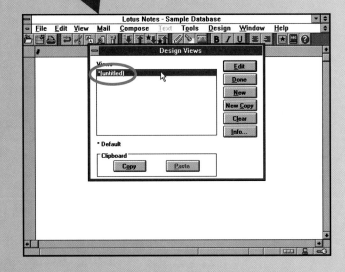

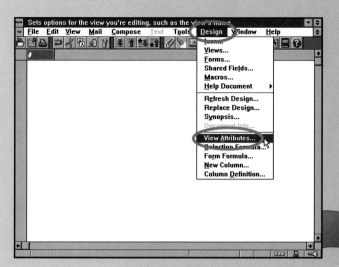

4 Click **Design** on the Notes menu bar, and then click **View Attributes** to display the Design View Attributes dialog box.

5 Enter a title for the view in the Name text box. For this task, type **New View**.

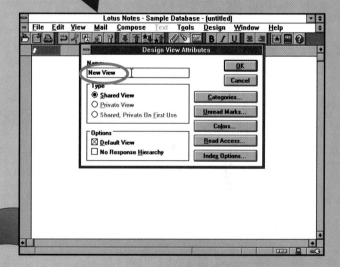

6 Click the **OK** button to close the Design View Attributes dialog box.

Task 43: Creating a View

7 Double-click the gray space to the right of the # sign to display the Design Column Definition dialog box.

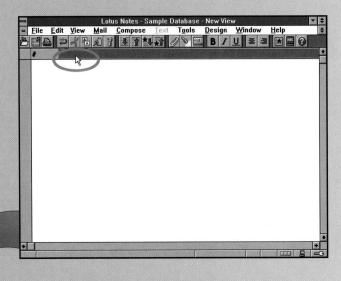

8 Enter a title for the column in the **Title** text box. For this task, type **Subject Column**.

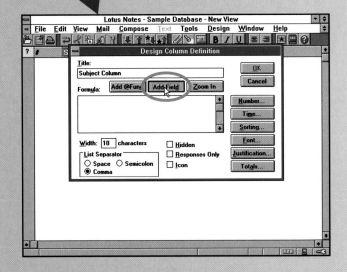

9 Click the **Add Field** button to display the list of available fields to place in the column.

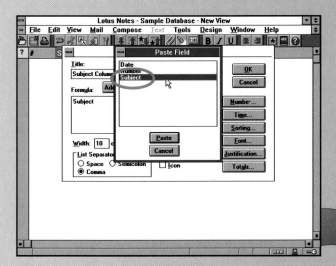

10 In the Paste Field dialog box, select the field you want to add to the column by double-clicking it. For this task, select the **Subject** field.

11 In the Design Column Definition dialog box, click the **OK** button to save the column definition.

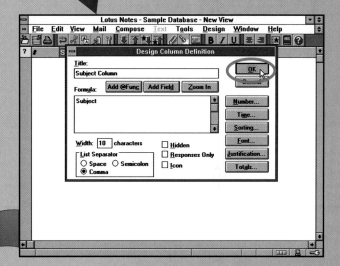

12 Add two more columns to your view that represent additional fields in the form(s) you have created for your database.

155

Task 43: Creating a View

13 To save the new view, click **File** on the Notes menu bar, and then click **Save** to save the new form.

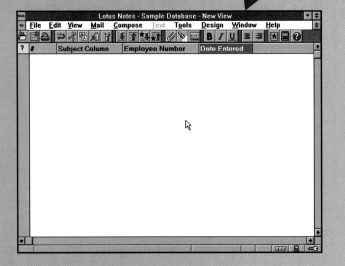

14 To exit the view, double-click it with your *right* mouse button.

Viewing and Changing Access Levels of Databases

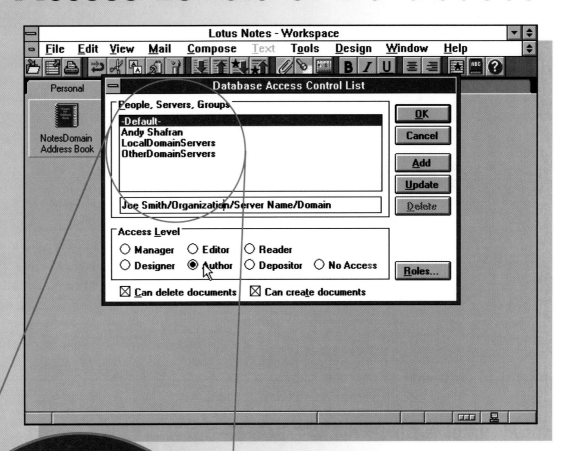

"Why would I do this?"

Now that you have the backbone of your new database created (forms and views), you need to think about database security. Although database access levels may not be important for databases on your local machine, they are crucial for databases on a Notes server. Controlling database security levels can become complicated and confusing.

This task shows you how to check access security levels for databases.

Task 44: Viewing and Changing Access Levels of Databases

1 From your Notes workspace, select the database for which you want to check security levels by clicking its database icon.

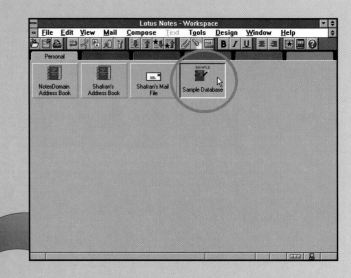

2 Click **File** on the Notes menu bar, and then click **Database**. Then click **Access Control** to display the Database Access Control List dialog box.

3 Type the full name and domain of the user you want to add to the Database Access Control List in the text box.

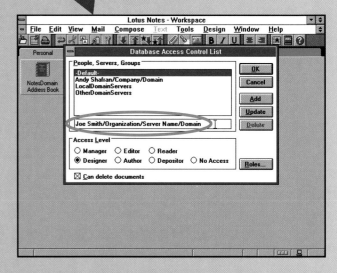

Task 44: Viewing and Changing Access Levels of Databases

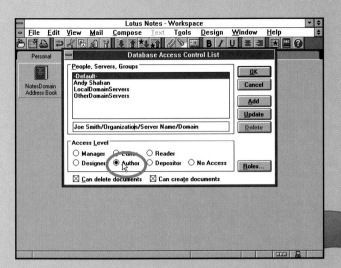

4 Select the access level you want to give to the user by clicking the appropriate radio button in the Access Level area.

NOTE ▼

To change the access level of a user who is already defined in the ACL list, highlight the user's name in the People, Servers, Groups box, and then select a new radio button from the Access Level area. Click the Update button for the change to take affect.

5 Click the **Add** button to add the user to the Database Access Control List.

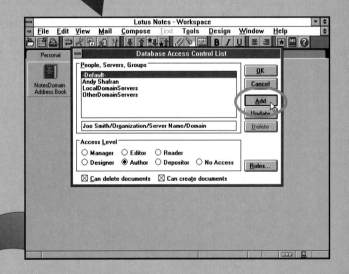

6 When you are finished adding users to the Database Access Control List, click the **OK** button to save the updated list.

PART VIII

Advanced Notes Features

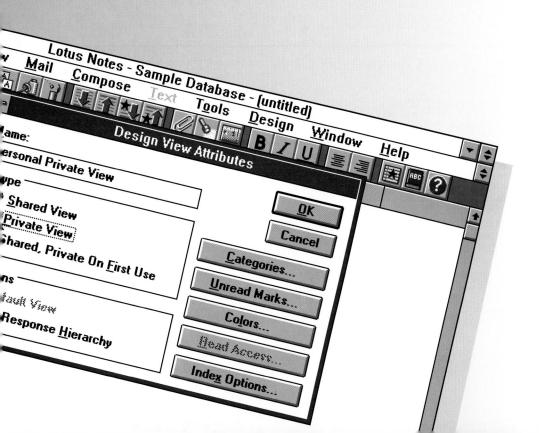

Part VIII: Advanced Notes Features

Now that you are familiar with most of the basics of Lotus Notes, it is time to learn how to take advantage of some of its advanced features. With Notes, not only can you send messages and documents back and forth between databases, but you can also exchange files. By enabling you to attach files to any document, Notes can be a file and document management software package. Other advanced features of Notes include doc links and pop-ups. This part also discusses creating private views.

A doc link allows you to access other Notes documents from one document. Depicted as small icons, doc links act as pointers to other Notes documents. Using doc links, you can display other Notes documents from any database within your Notes network. For example, NotesHelp uses doc links on a regular basis as pointers to other entries on the same issue. Doc links are also automatically created when you use the reply form to respond to a piece of NotesMail. In the reply form, a doc link is created that refers to the original memo. By clicking the doc link icon (which looks like a small document) in the reply form, you can access your original memo.

Notes also has the ability to store complete files in documents. You can use this feature to mail files to other users, create file libraries, or to send presentations to your colleagues. You can send files to other Notes users. For example, a programmer can write and compile a program using his own software. He can send his executable program as a file attachment to another Notes user so that user can detach and run the program. Notes allows you to send any type of file via file attachments.

In addition, you can also import data into Notes. Text files created with a word processor can be imported as actual Notes data. For example, if you have an employee manual typed in a word processor, you can import the text so that other Notes users can see the information on-line, without having to open another program. Notes can import files from a wide variety of text and data types.

When you are creating documents, you may need to add a note about certain text. In Lotus Notes, you accomplish this task by using pop-ups. *Pop-ups* are pieces of added text that you access by using your mouse. You can usually spot text that has a pop-up associated with it because the text is usually surrounded with a green box on your Notes screen.

In addition to attaching files to Notes documents, you can also import various file types as well. Using Notes, you can import bit-mapped images, Lotus 1-2-3 worksheets, text files, and many other file types. You can mail this imported information or store it in a database.

There are two types of views in Lotus Notes. You have already learned how to create regular views that are accessible for everyone who can access a database. This section shows you how to create a private view that only you can access. The private view is stored on your workstation as opposed to the Notes server.

This part shows you how to use pop-ups, doc links, private views, and other advanced features of Notes.

Using Doc Links

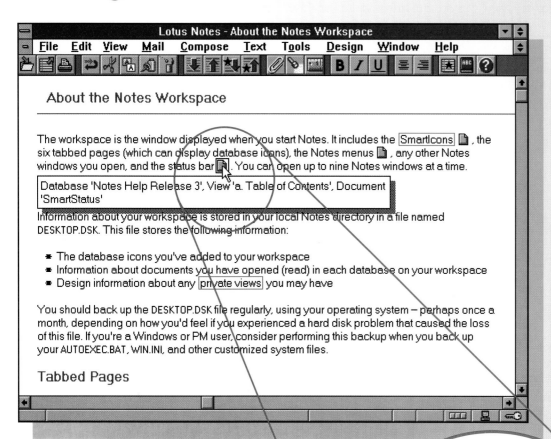

"Why would I do this?"

Doc links help documents reference each other. A doc link is a small icon that displays another document when you click it. Doc links can be used to reference documents from within the same database or from any database on your Notes network. Doc links are also built into NotesHelp.

This task shows you how to recognize and use doc links to reference other documents.

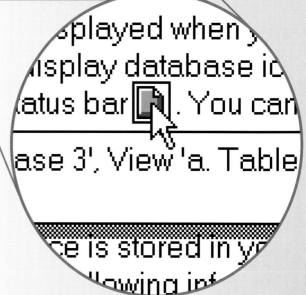

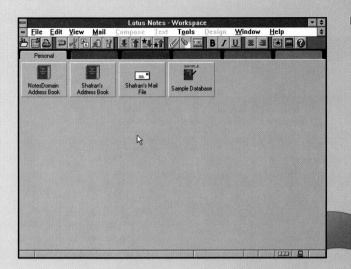

1 From the Notes workspace, press the **F1** key to display the NotesHelp screen.

2 Double-click the small icon that looks like a page to display the referenced document to that portion of NotesHelp. Holding down the left mouse button while the mouse pointer is on the icon displays the title of the linked document, as shown in the figure.

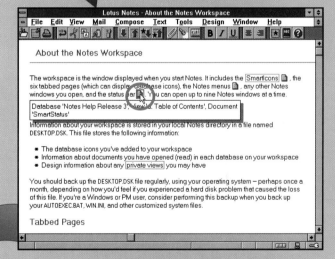

3 Double-click with your *right* mouse button to exit from the NotesHelp screens.

Making Doc Links

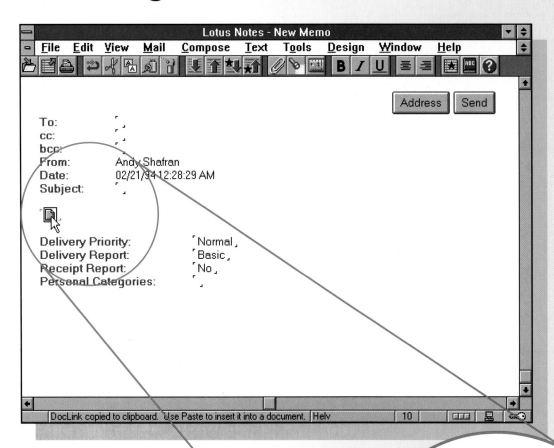

"Why would I do this?"

Not only are doc links easy to use, they are also easy to create. When you reply to mail messages, for example, Notes automatically creates a doc link from the original message to the reply.

This task shows you how to create a doc link to reference another Notes document.

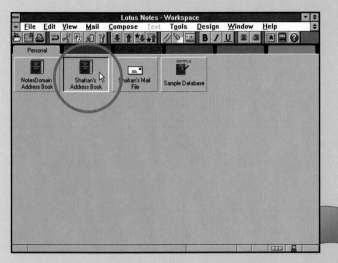

1 Open the database that contains the message to be linked.

2 Open the document you want to link by double-clicking it from your view.

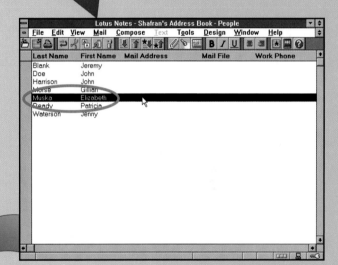

3 Create the doc link by clicking **Edit** on the menu bar and then clicking **Make DocLink**.

Task 46: Making Doc Links

4 Edit your to-be-linked document and compose the document you want to place the doc link into. For this task, click **Mail** on the Notes menu bar, click **Compose**, and then click **Memo**.

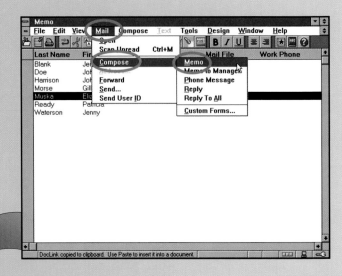

5 In the desired rich text field, click the **Paste** SmartIcon to paste the doc link into your document.

6 Double-click the doc link icon to access the document you have linked.

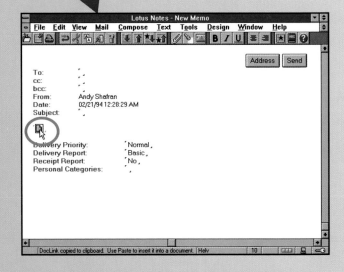

Creating File Attachments

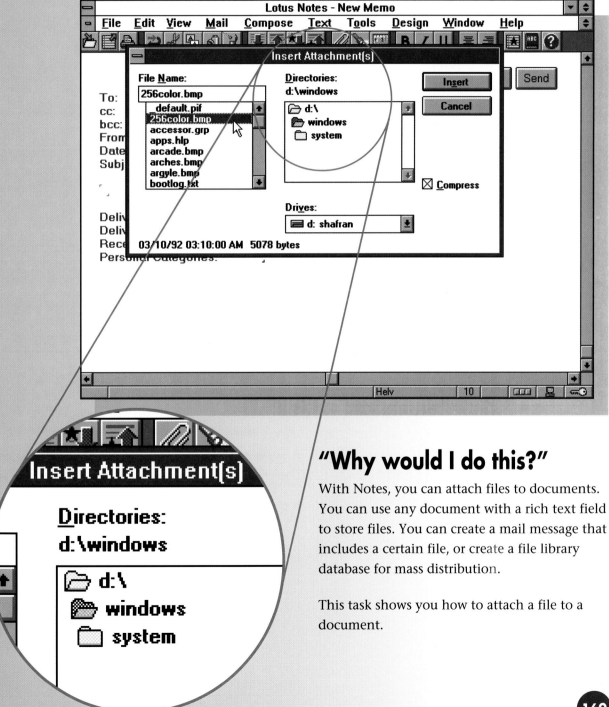

"Why would I do this?"

With Notes, you can attach files to documents. You can use any document with a rich text field to store files. You can create a mail message that includes a certain file, or create a file library database for mass distribution.

This task shows you how to attach a file to a document.

Task 47: Creating File Attachments

1 Click **Compose** on the Notes menu bar, and then click the kind of document you want to attach to a file to select it. For this task, click **Mail** on the Notes menu bar, click **Compose**, and then click **Memo**.

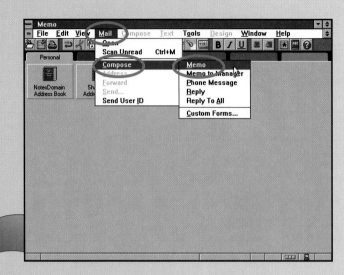

2 In the document, click the field to which you want to attach a file.

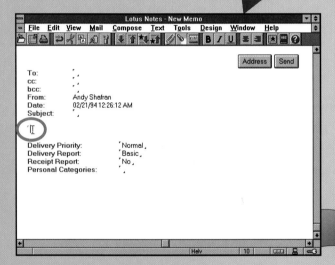

> **NOTE** ▼
>
> You can attach files to rich text fields only.

3 Click the **Attach** SmartIcon (the paper clip) to display the Insert Attachment dialog box.

> **NOTE** ▼
>
> You can also attach a file by clicking **File** on the menu bar and then clicking **Attach**.

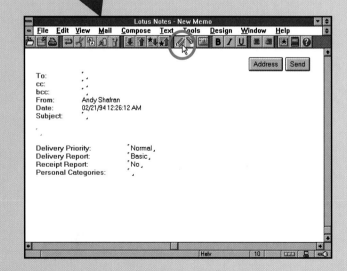

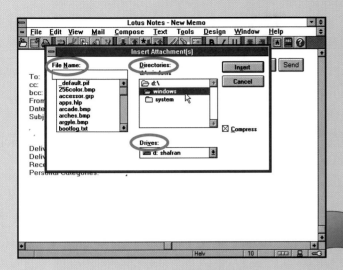

4 Use the **Drives**, **Directories**, and **File Name** scroll boxes to find the file you want to attach to your document.

5 Select the file you want to attach by clicking it.

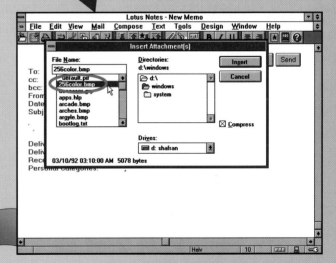

6 Click the **Insert** button to insert the file in your document.

171

TASK 48
Inserting a Pop-Up

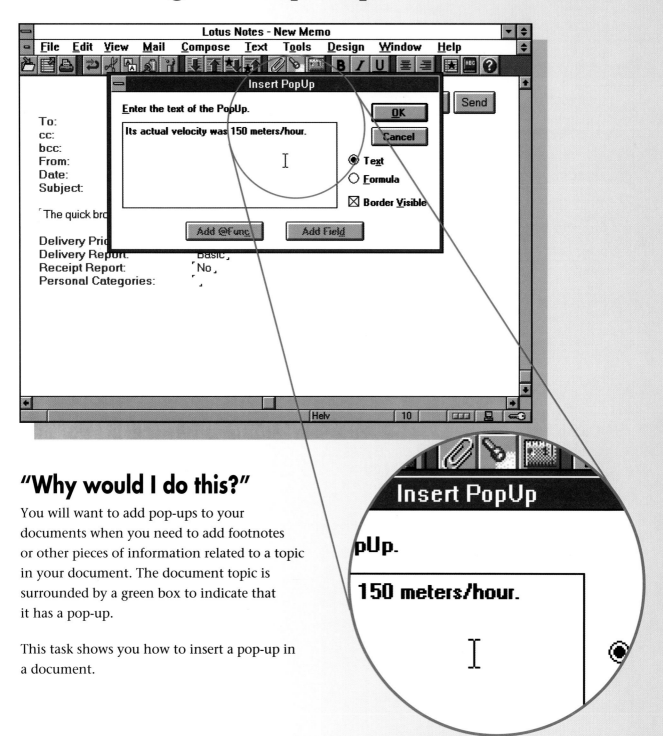

"Why would I do this?"

You will want to add pop-ups to your documents when you need to add footnotes or other pieces of information related to a topic in your document. The document topic is surrounded by a green box to indicate that it has a pop-up.

This task shows you how to insert a pop-up in a document.

Task 48: Inserting a Pop-Up

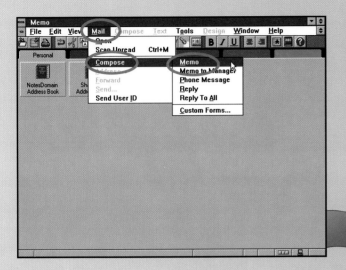

1 Click the **Compose** menu on the Notes menu bar, and then click the kind of document you want insert a pop-up in to select it. For this task, click **Mail** on the menu bar, click **Compose**, and then click **Memo**.

2 Type the text you want in the correct fields.

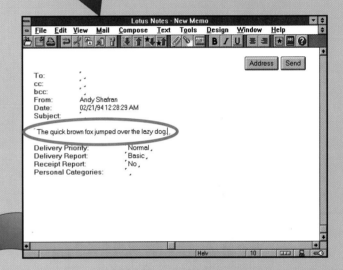

3 Select the text you want to create a pop-up around by clicking it.

Task 48: Inserting a Pop-Up

4 Click **Edit** from the Notes menu bar, and then click **Insert**. Click **PopUp** to display the Insert PopUp dialog box.

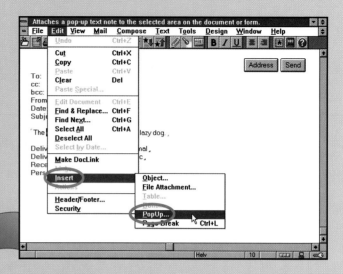

5 Enter the text you want to appear in the pop-up window when it's activated.

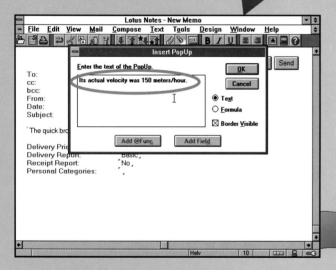

6 Click the **OK** button to save the pop-up text.

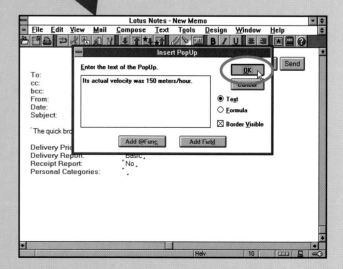

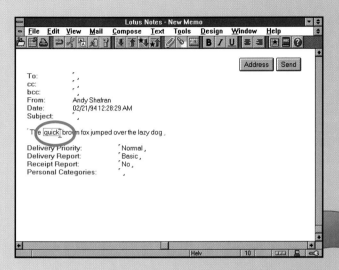

7 The text that has a related pop-up now appears in your document with a green box surrounding it. You cannot view a pop-up in a field while in edit mode.

8 After saving your document, enter it again so you are in read mode. In read mode, you can view the text in your pop-up.

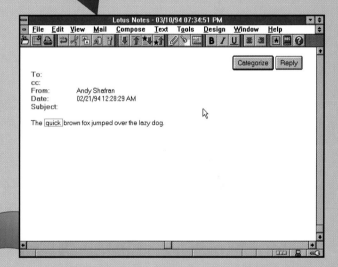

9 Click and hold your left mouse button anywhere in the green box of the pop-up to view your inserted text.

Importing Data

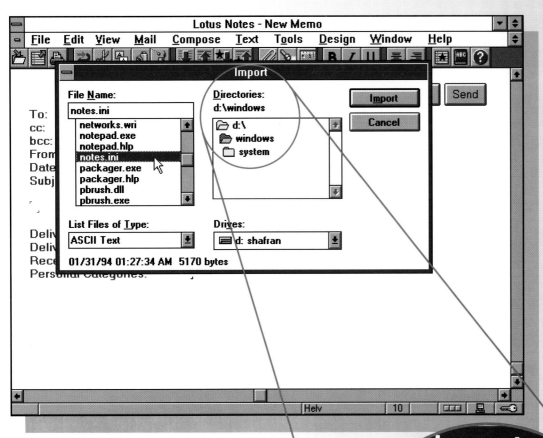

"Why would I do this?"

Notes documents can handle graphics, text, and multimedia files. Notes can import any Windows-supported file type into a Notes document. If you want to send an editable file to a colleague but don't want to attach it to a document, you can import the text into a document.

This task shows you how to import a simple text file into a Notes document.

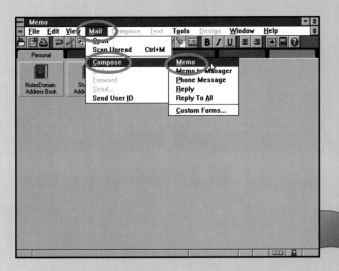

1 Click the **Compose** menu on the Notes menu bar, and then click the kind of document into which you want to import text. For this task, click **Mail** on the menu bar, click **Compose**, and then click **Memo**.

2 Select the field you want to import your file into and click **File** from the Notes menu bar; then click **Import** to display the Import dialog box.

> **NOTE** ▼
>
> To import text, you must be in a rich text field in your document.

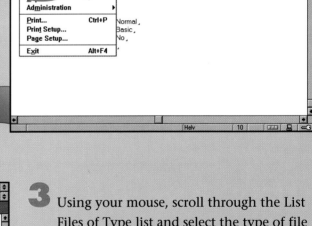

3 Using your mouse, scroll through the List Files of Type list and select the type of file you want to import.

Task 49: Importing Data

4 Use the **Drives**, **Directories**, and **File Name** scroll boxes to find the file you want to import.

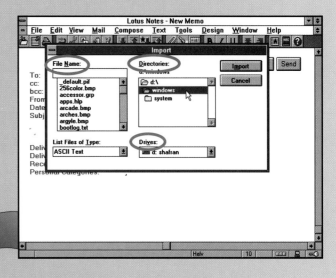

5 Select the file you want to import by clicking it.

6 Click the **Import** button to insert the file in your document.

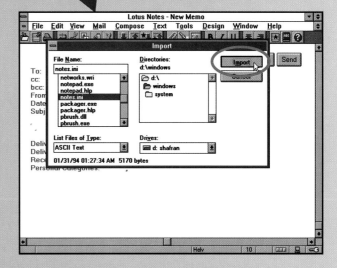

TASK 50

Creating a Private View

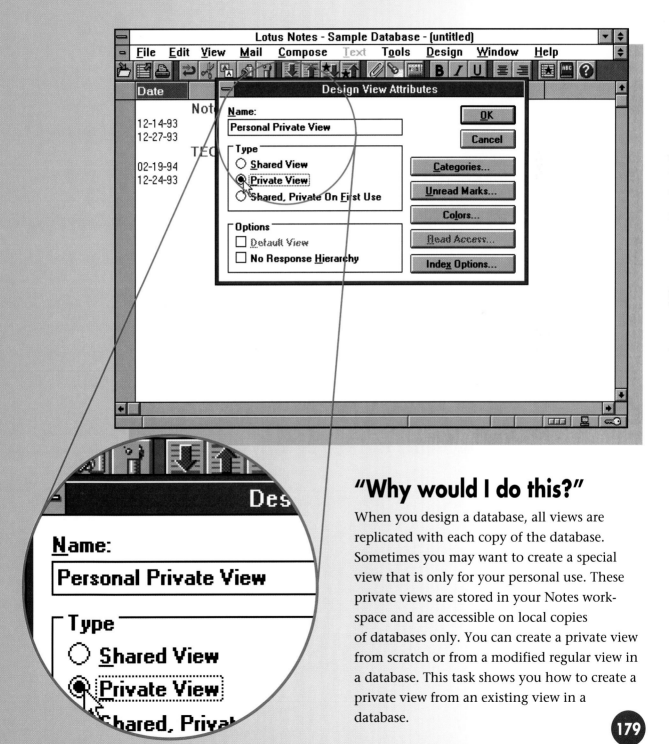

"Why would I do this?"

When you design a database, all views are replicated with each copy of the database. Sometimes you may want to create a special view that is only for your personal use. These private views are stored in your Notes workspace and are accessible on local copies of databases only. You can create a private view from scratch or from a modified regular view in a database. This task shows you how to create a private view from an existing view in a database.

179

Task 50: Creating a Private View

1 Open a database to which you have at least Reader access so you can edit the existing views.

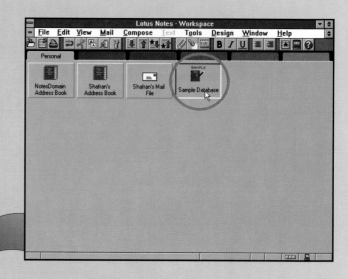

2 Click **Design** on the Notes menu bar, and then click **Views** to display the Design Views dialog box.

3 Highlight the view you want to make a private view copy of by clicking it.

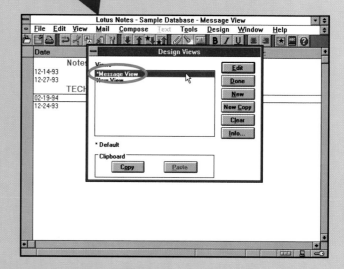

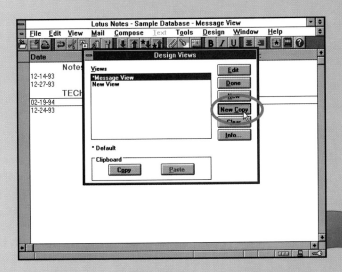

4 Click the **New Copy** button to create a new copy of that view.

5 Click **Design** on the Notes menu bar, and then click **View Attributes** to display the Design View Attributes dialog box.

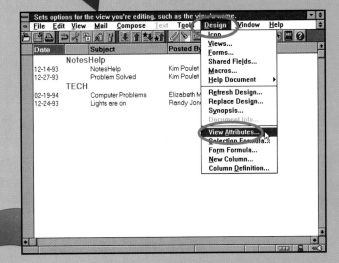

6 Enter the name of the view in the Name box.

Task 50: Creating a Private View

7 Click the **Private View** radio button in the Type area to select it.

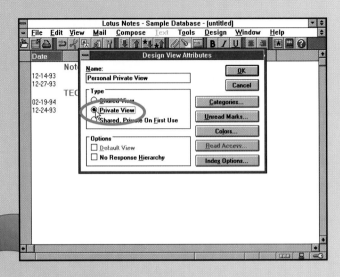

8 Click the **OK** button to save the view information.

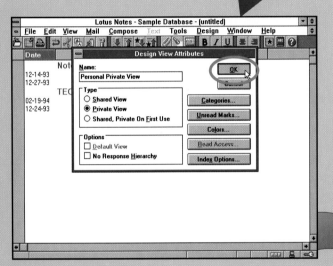

9 Click **File** on the Notes menu bar, and then click **Save** to save the new private view.

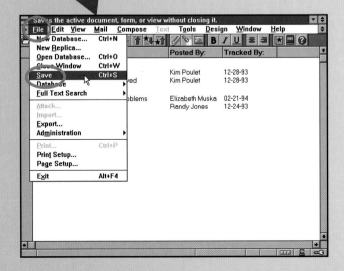

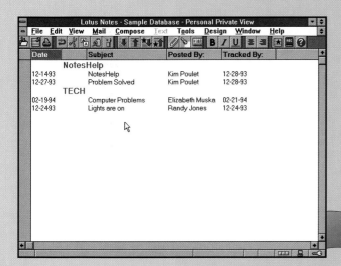

10 Double-click with your *right* mouse button to exit the view edit mode.

11 Click **View** on the menu bar, and select your new private view.

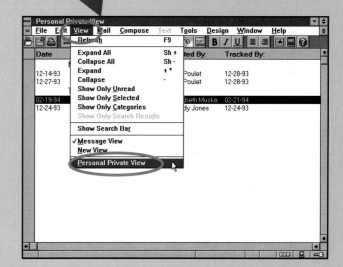

Glossary

ACL (Access Control List)   The list of allowed users for a database. Lists who is allowed to access the database and what kind of access they have. Access can range from No Access to Manager.

application   A single Notes database, or a linked collection of databases, created and designed to serve a particular need.

attachment   A file included in a Notes document. To send a file to another Notes user, you can send the file as an attachment in an e-mail message.

BCC (Blind Carbon Copy)   Sends a copy of an e-mail message to a recipient(s) in the BCC field without any of the other recipients being aware of it.

button   Rectangular area on a form that the user can click to perform Notes menu commands or to execute a formula. The form's designer can place a button almost anywhere on the form; the user can place a button inside of any rich text field.

CC (Carbon Copy)   Sends a copy of the e-mail message to the recipient(s) in the CC field.

client   Computer or workstation at your desk. Also refers to the user, you!

database   A Notes file, represented by a database icon. Databases store documents. Typically, databases are located on servers and accessed by clients from all over the LAN.

database icon   Rectangular icon which represents a Notes database with a picture and descriptive title. Optionally, the file name and server location can be displayed on the icon.

design   The design (or design elements) of a database defines how the users read, input, and modify information in a database. The design elements of a database are fields, forms, views, and macros.

desktop   See *workspace*.

doc link   A small page icon that displays a referenced document when double-clicked.

document   A form that contains specific information in its fields.

field   A place on a document where information is stored. Fields are logically grouped in documents by a form. Some fields allow you to type into them, and others have formulas that perform calculations.

folder   Space on the desktop containing database icons. Also called a page.

form   The design of a document. This determines how fields are displayed and how information can be inputted into them.

full text index   A listing of all words in the database for use in full text searches.

full text search   A query against the full text index to locate records matching specified words, phrases, numbers, or dates.

groupware   An application that helps people work collaboratively with electronic information. Lotus Notes is an example of groupware.

GUI (Graphical User Interface)   What you see on-screen. The menus, SmartIcons, buttons, and the workspace are all part of the interface. The behavior of the menus, and of the mouse, is also part of the interface.

LAN (Local Area Network)   Servers and clients connected by wires for the purpose of sharing data. The servers typically stay logged on to the LAN, so that their databases can be accessed at any time. Clients typically log on and off of the LAN as necessary.

laptop   A portable computer, often used as a remote workstation.

modem   A device that attaches to a computer to allow for remote communication via phone lines.

Name & Address Book (N&A Book)   A database (and an application) containing the names of all the Notes users on the network. Notes uses this database to route mail.

page   See *folder*.

Part IX: Glossary

password   Encrypted text string that denies use of User ID to unauthorized persons. Typically, Notes users each have a single User ID, which they do not share.

pop-up   Area on a form that you can click for additional information. The form's designer can place pop-ups almost anywhere on the form; the user can place a pop-up in any rich text field. Usually, you see pop-ups as a green rectangle surrounding text.

private view   A view made specifically for you. Regular views are stored on the server; private views are stored in the desktop.dsk file on your workstation.

record   See *document*.

remote workstation   A computer that connects to the network via modem.

server   A computer that stores data for use by clients. In Notes, the server also authenticates your User ID when you attempt to access the server; you must have a User ID in order to access any server. Notes databases are typically located on servers.

SmartIcons   A row of small square icons (default location is at the top of the screen) that you can click to perform Notes menu commands.

template   A database without records. You can use templates as a starting point when creating a new database because they contain a complete set of design elements. Notes comes packaged with many templates; you can see a list of these templates by choosing File from the menu bar, and then choosing New Database.

User ID   A file that contains an encrypted, unique ID allowing the owner of the file access to Notes servers and databases. This file is often protected with a password.

view (shared view)   A display of documents in a database. Views contain documents that are sorted, totaled, or grouped together in almost any logical manner.

workspace   Window displayed when Notes is first activated. The workspace has six tabbed pages, or folders. You can view different folders by clicking the tabs at the top of the screen.

Index

Index

Index

U

V

W-Z